AF622713

Ukraine Youth
Between Days

Daniel King

DAMIANI

Ukraine Youth
Between Days

Daniel King

Introduction by
Christopher Niquet

When photographed in the anonymous space of a studio, abstracted from their surroundings and the city of Kiev where they grew up, the teenagers in Daniel King's photographs could be your neighbors, your nieces or nephews. They could come from London, Berlin, Paris or New York. But the white paper background is just a moment, a pause, a break. Almost a dream. They are here and there, present and absent. They are young adults in their most formative years. Like every generation before them, they are both the negative and positive of all feelings. They carry within them the possibilities their parents have only dreamt of – they are the first teenagers born in Ukraine after 1991.

Look deeply into the frail, blond, teenage girl's eyes. She fights the wind, holding her wavy hair out of her face with skinny, long fingers delicate like bird claws. She is singular and yet she is so much. She could be the young girl on a 1950s propaganda poster, the cliché of communist youth, the idealistic image of pure thoughts and pure body. Except the out-of-focus space behind her isn't a blue lake in the countryside. The wall is being painted with revolutionary slogans. Her hands look crippled, and you can see the tension as she holds that long, angelic, blond hair. She isn't just a stereotype of the pretty, young, Eastern European girl; she is also its negative reflection. She is the young boy photographed by Diane Arbus playing war in a New York park in 1962 holding a toy grenade in each hand, mimicking the fear that he saw in the Vietnam war reports on television. His expression is a mixture of playfulness and defiance. And, she is also the teenage gang member photographed by Bruce Davidson in a Brooklyn subway station in 1965, provocatively brushing her hair, her back to us, her shirt unbuttoned and untucked. A glimpse of her face is reflected in the mirror while her boyfriend rolls up the sleeves of his T-shirt next to her. Is she washing away the clues of a carefree afternoon before returning home to her parents? Is she a good girl lost in the thoughts of her changing identity?

We can't know for sure who Adelina is. She is changing and that image of her is both soothing and reassuring, proof that in the midst of this city in turmoil you can preserve some innocence, or at least the look of it. As pure as she looks, you also know that the events taking place around her will change her. But how? Will she be a grenade-throwing revolutionary, or will she grow to be a teenage girl merely preoccupied by boys?

Look deeper into Kristina's sharp, dark, staring eyes. There is no shyness. She is looking at us. Her face emerges from the dark shadows of the trees around her. She is completely exposed, her bangs cut short on her forehead. Her shirt is closed all the way to her throat – the perfect frame for her delicate, fearless but tense features. She, too, carries the duality of teenagers. Move her face back a few centimeters and she is now buried in the dark shadows. She is the Sally Mann image of a twelve-year old American girl, curled up on the hood of an old car with the word 'doom' painted on it, clutching a butterfly net. You want to believe that she is simply tired of running through fields chasing specimens for her collection but maybe she is just remembering an afternoon of bliss spent as a younger girl, before the teenage blues swiped her. Maybe she is a runaway child whose only reminder of a happy past is this butterfly net she can't seem to let go of. She is static yet unmovable like Ed van Der Elsken's picture of a dark-haired girl sitting on a Paris bench in 1954. The rain isn't going to make her move. Her clothing is wet. Her eyes are painted black. The day is rising. She is smoking her last cigarette. You cannot imagine anyone taking her out of this spot against her will. Whether she just sat down or has been there for hours, you know that she is there by choice.

All of these images are visual representations of youth's beauty and singularity, the yearning for unexplored feelings, territories and people, coupled with the innate knowledge that we are all the same, no matter how different we may seem.

Youth has always been a determining part of every population's road to freedom, their idealism so strong and communicable that they can take down governments. With their raw, irrepressible emotions, they have the capacity to convince others that this is a time for change, to make their feelings universalities. Remember the revolts of May 1968 in France: a movement that started with the students of the Sorbonne and their concerns about class discrimination in French society. They started a national movement that spread to workers and intellectuals and eventually led to the dissolution of the National Assembly.

Recall the desegregation experiment that started in 1957 at Central High School in Arkansas with the Little Rock Nine. That group of students, the first to be integrated into a white school, was confronted with a population that would rather have its schools shut down than open its doors to African-Americans. Their persistence in the face of the humiliations they had to face was a starting point for a wave of events that led to a new climate for social change.

The common denominator of all social movements is the idealism that comes from this feeling of indivisibility inherent to teenagers. It is an understanding that we are all equals and a fervent belief that a united group can leave its mark on society and catalyze evolution.

But with Kiev's youth we do not know the future developments that will inevitably shake them. And so we are left in a state of questioning. We look in their eyes, and we question whether the changes within them will be enough to change their country. We are able to see this because the photographer's role is instrumental to our perceptions of those teenagers.

We have all followed the news on what has happened and continues to happen since Daniel King left Kiev in mid-September 2013: the engagement of an entire population moved by new ideals and desires, the violence it reached and the political changes it brought.

Daniel King could have sensationalized his images and message. He could have come back to Kiev and documented the central square. He could have followed those teenagers and documented their daily lives in an agitated city. He chose instead to keep his focus on the little waves, the almost imperceptible changes in the people. He kept his focus on the invisible, the barely acknowledged. He left writing the end of the story to us.

These teenagers are a metaphor for the city they live in. They are destroying their identities as children and building their adult ones. They are taking over the parks, the public benches, the construction sites. They are like the plants and the graffiti, the billboards and posters. They are using the old to create the future.

Kiev is a city that is rooted deeply in its past, the older inhabitants appear almost like characters out of an Andrei Tarkovsky movie, dignified but out-of-touch peasants living in a maze of concrete.

Both the landscapes and the old seem impossibly rooted in the past: stale, not able to catch up with the present, maybe not even aware of the undercurrent of change that is taking over the city in which they live. Whether they are swimming by a construction site that was probably once just a pretty river bank or fishing in a lake filled with abandoned metallic structures, you wonder how they can keep their long traditions and not see how this place once so familiar has been changing. How can they be that oblivious to such signs?

The old statues standing in the park are no longer theirs. The young have made them their gathering spots. They have been stripped bare of their communist icons, concrete shapes without the looming presence of past leaders. They are no longer the symbols they used to be, but a kind of ground zero for the new ideas the young generation will come up with after an evening of drinking vodka alongside agitated debate. To the old they are no more than a signifier of their youth and the country's past, proof that they do not understand the changes happening around them. Silent reminders of how things used to be. For the young these places are the stepping stone to their new identities, a place to experiment with original ideas and thoughts.

Just like nature taking over remains of the past, youth is now shaping the new identity of Kiev.

– Christopher Niquet

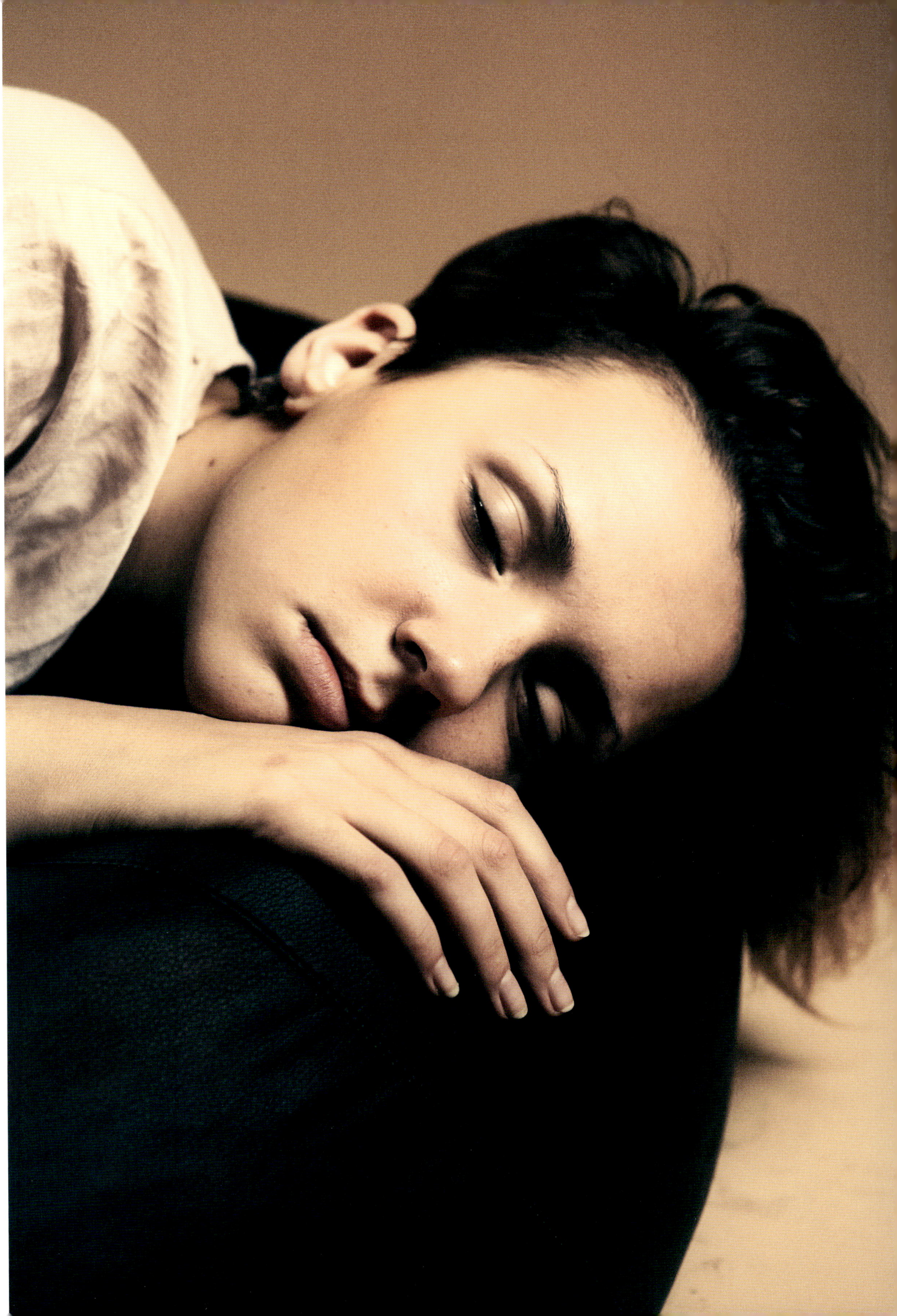

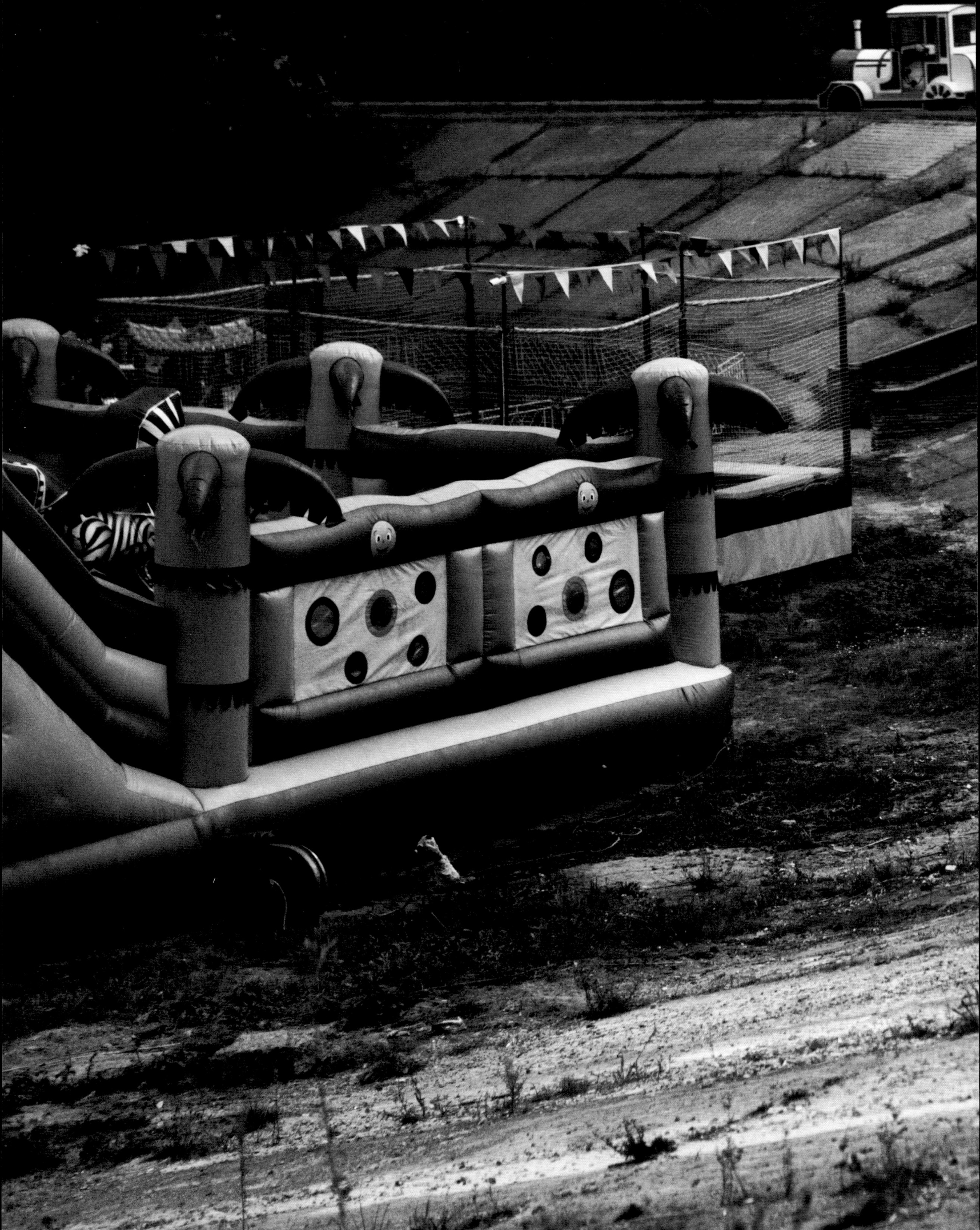

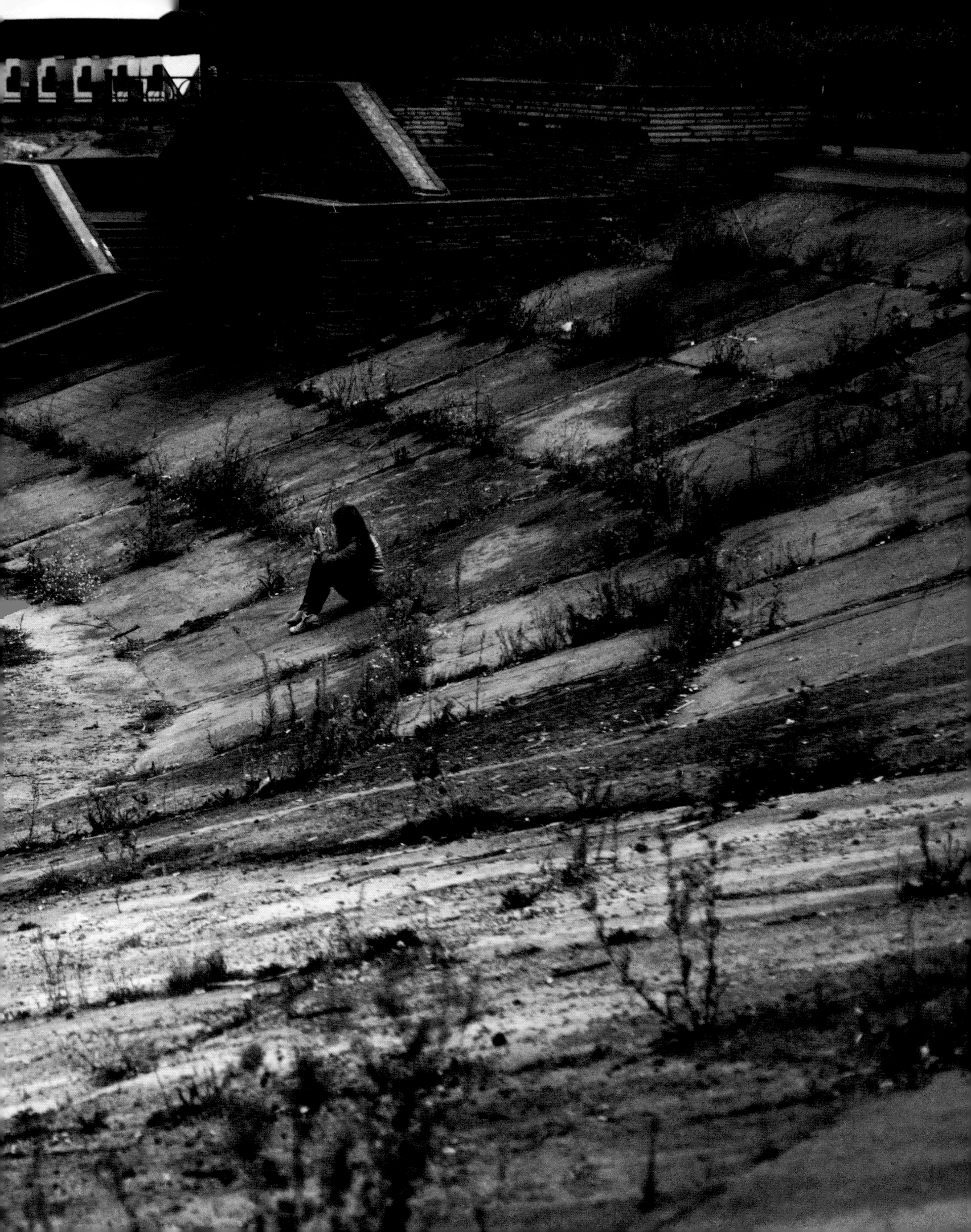

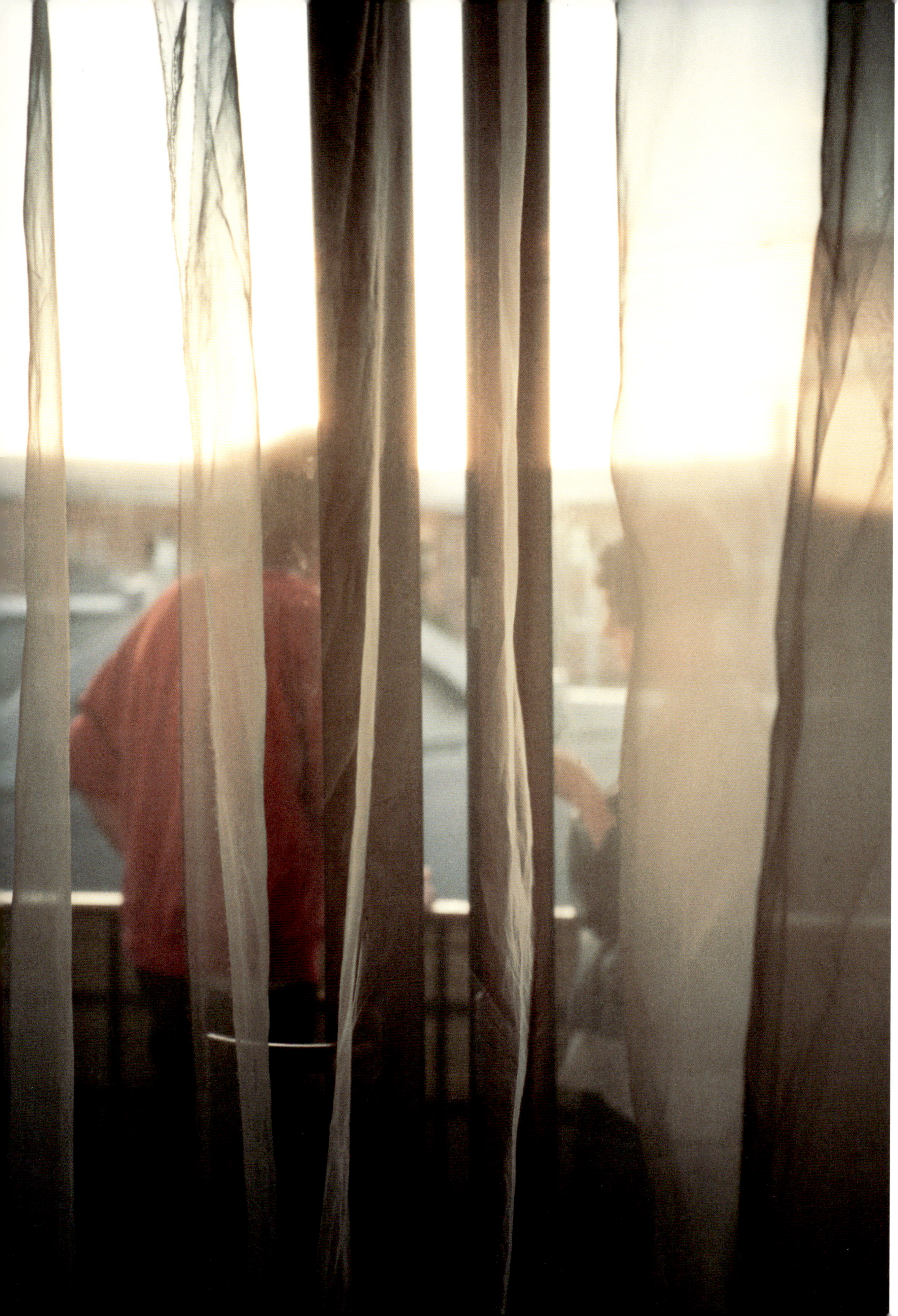

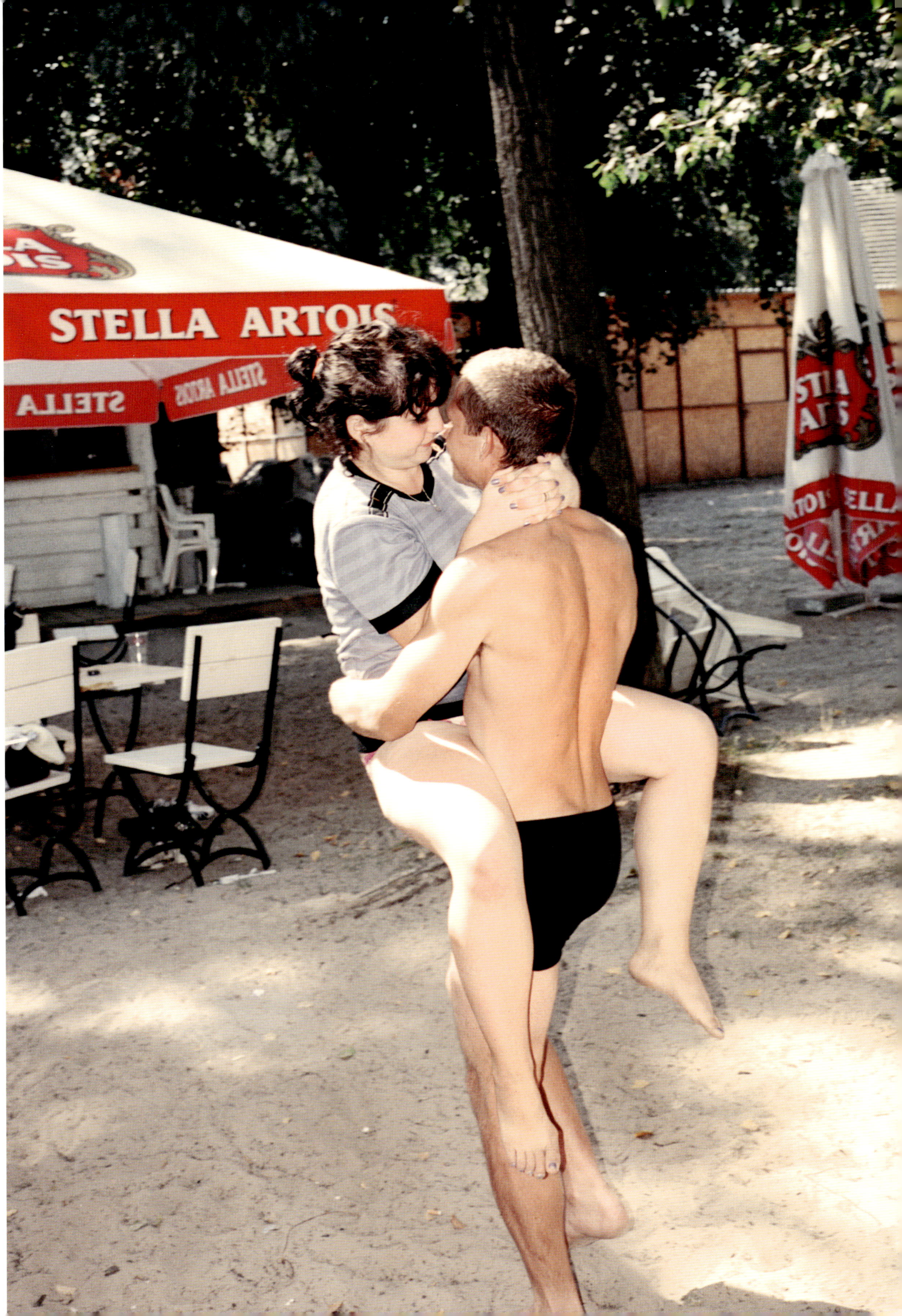
STELLA ARTOIS

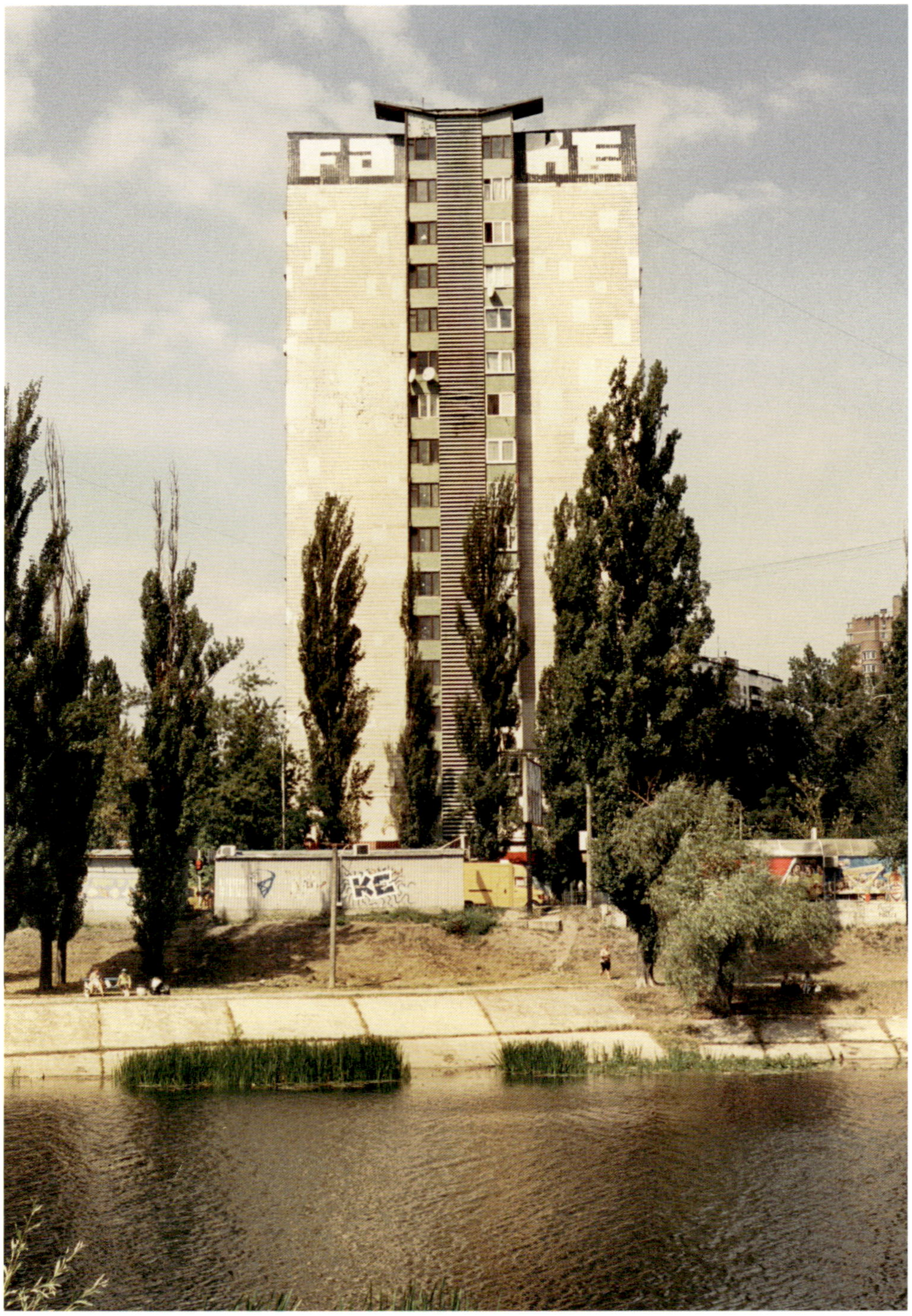
Fa KE
KE

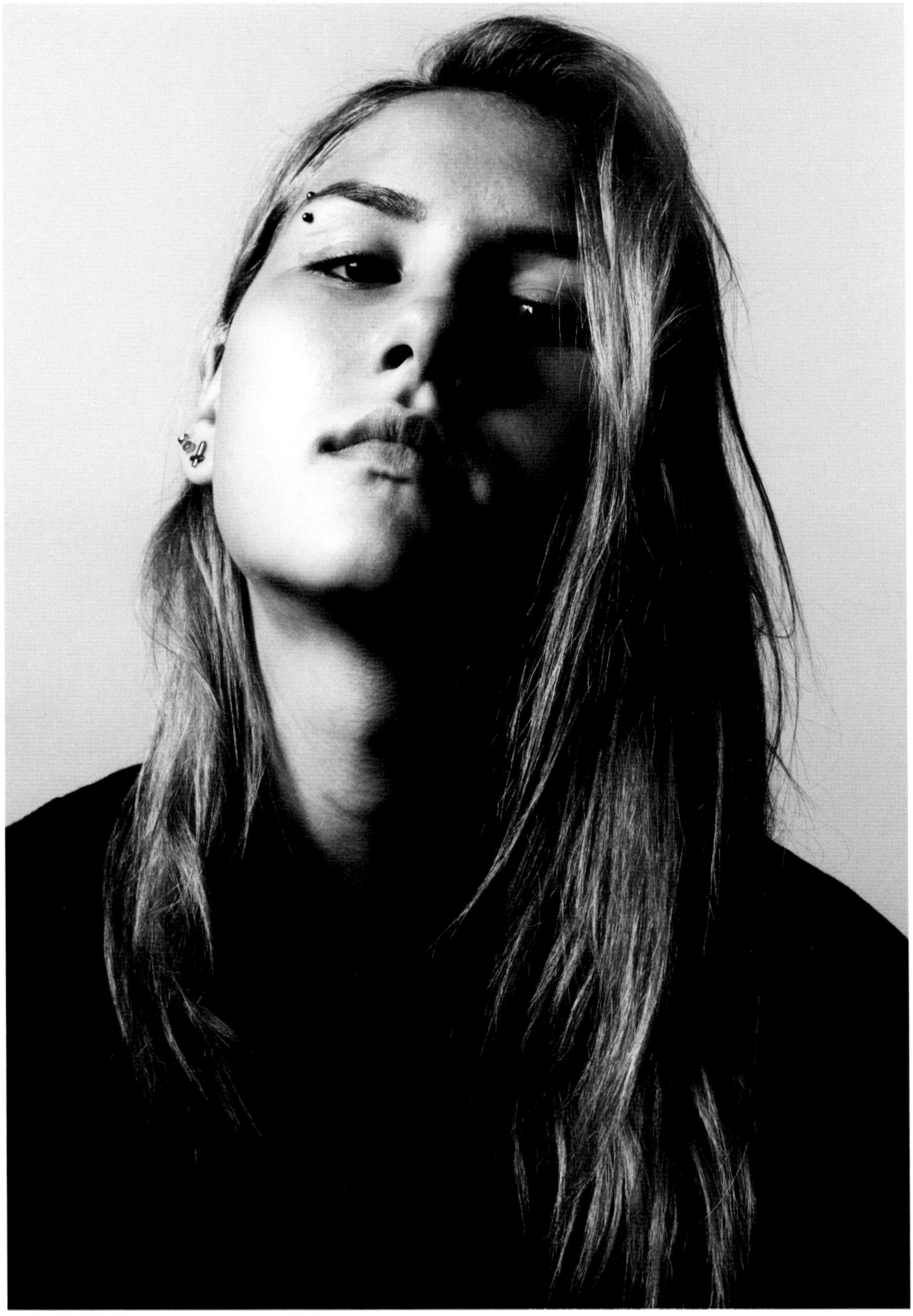

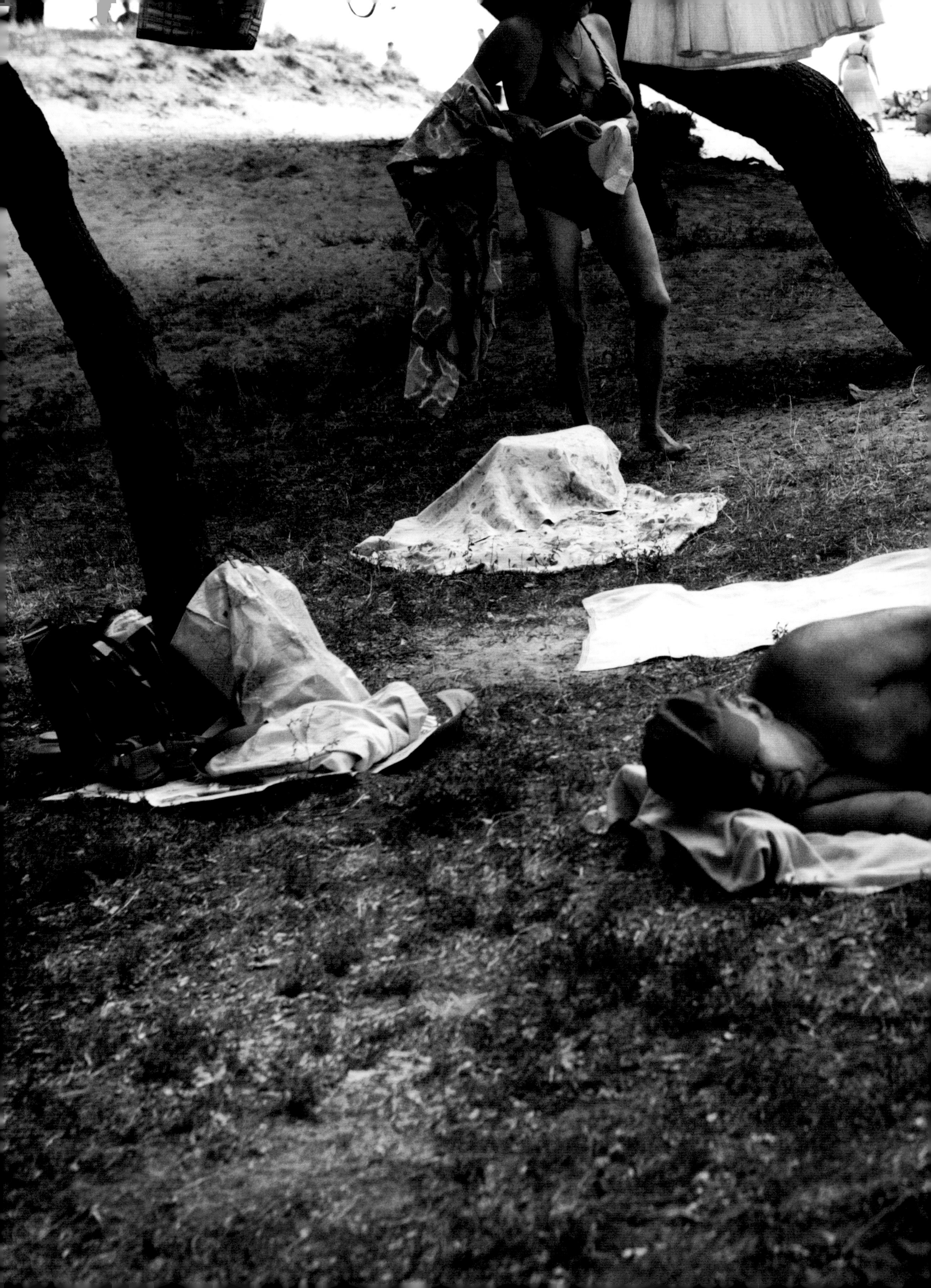

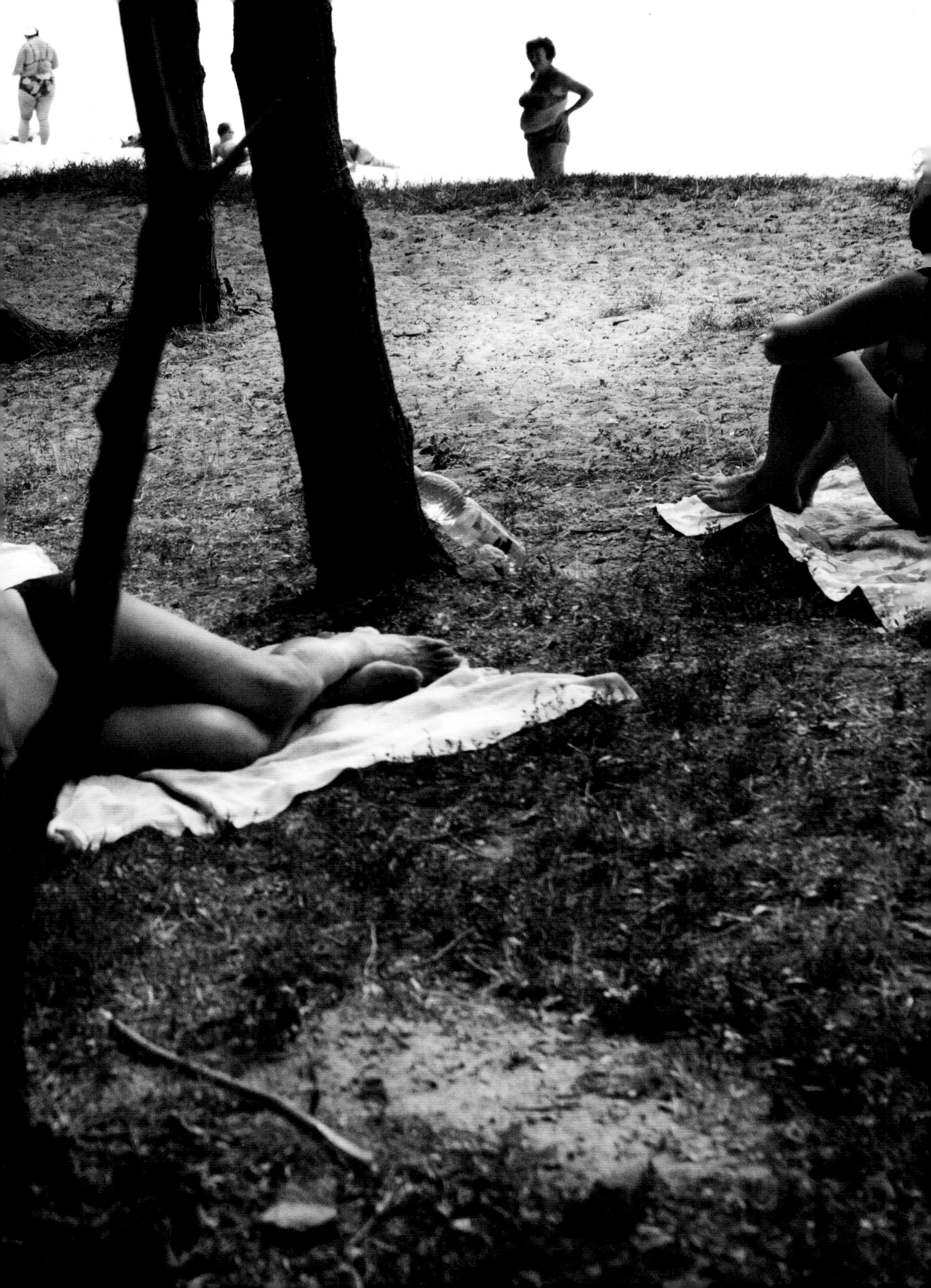

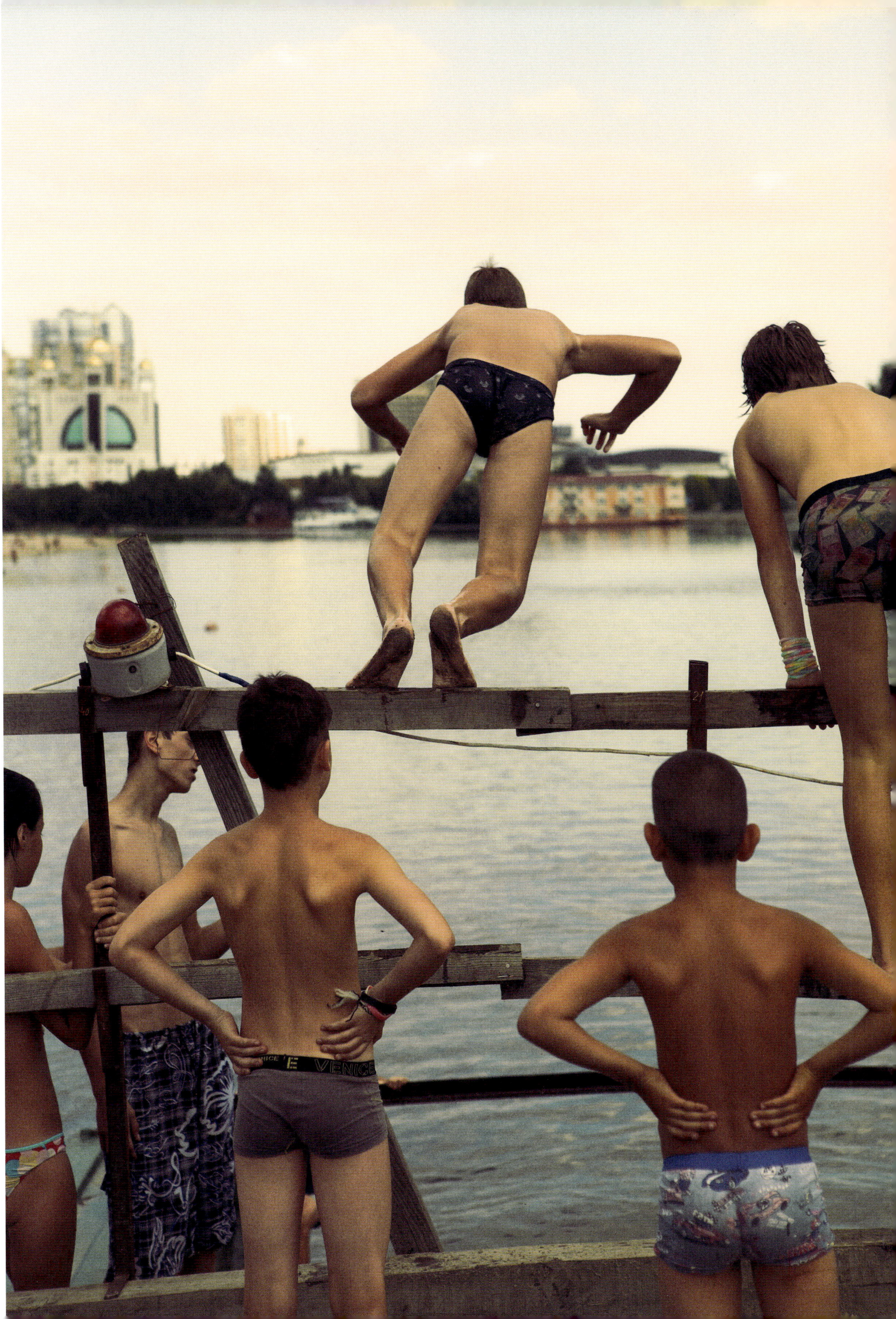

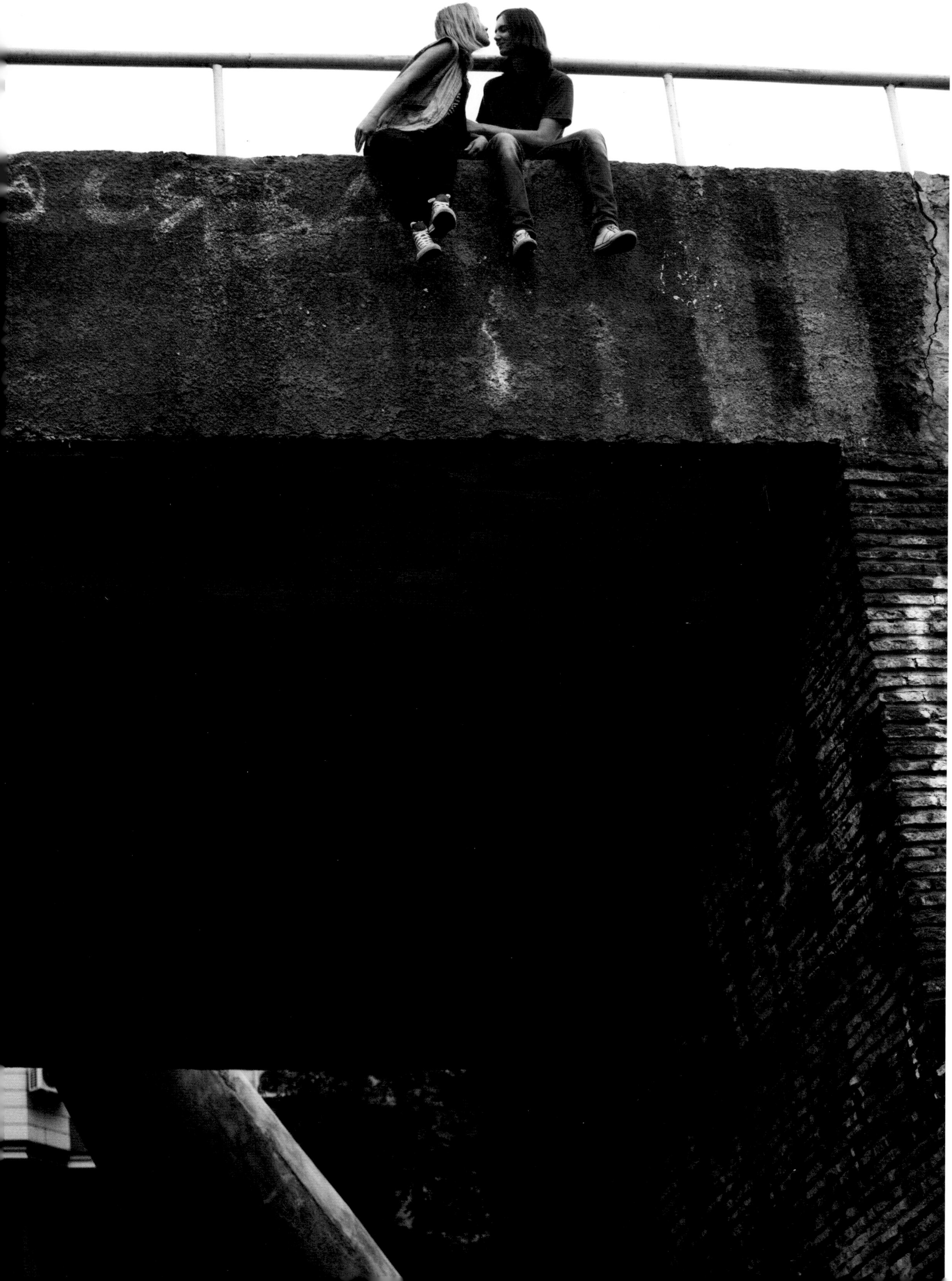

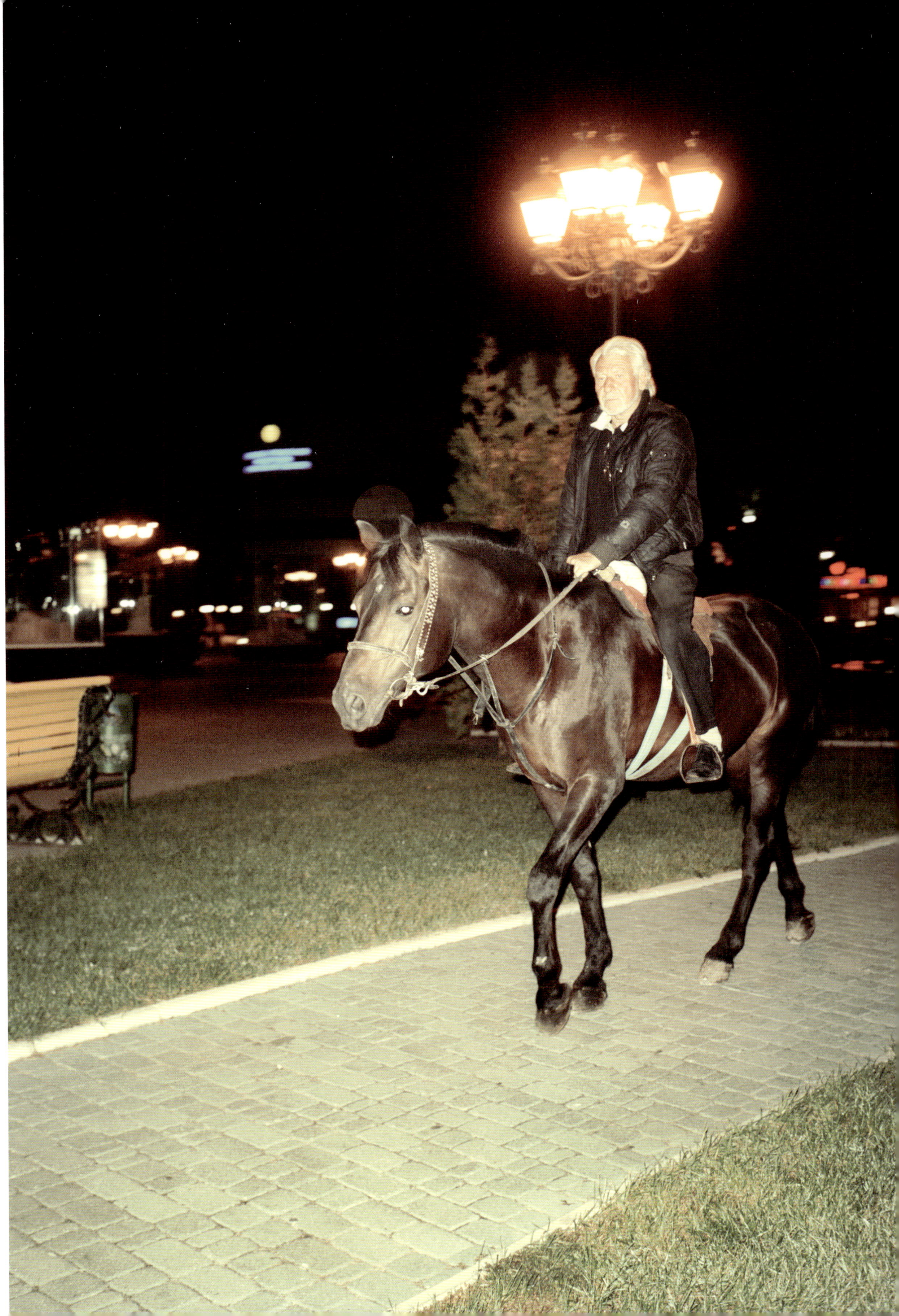

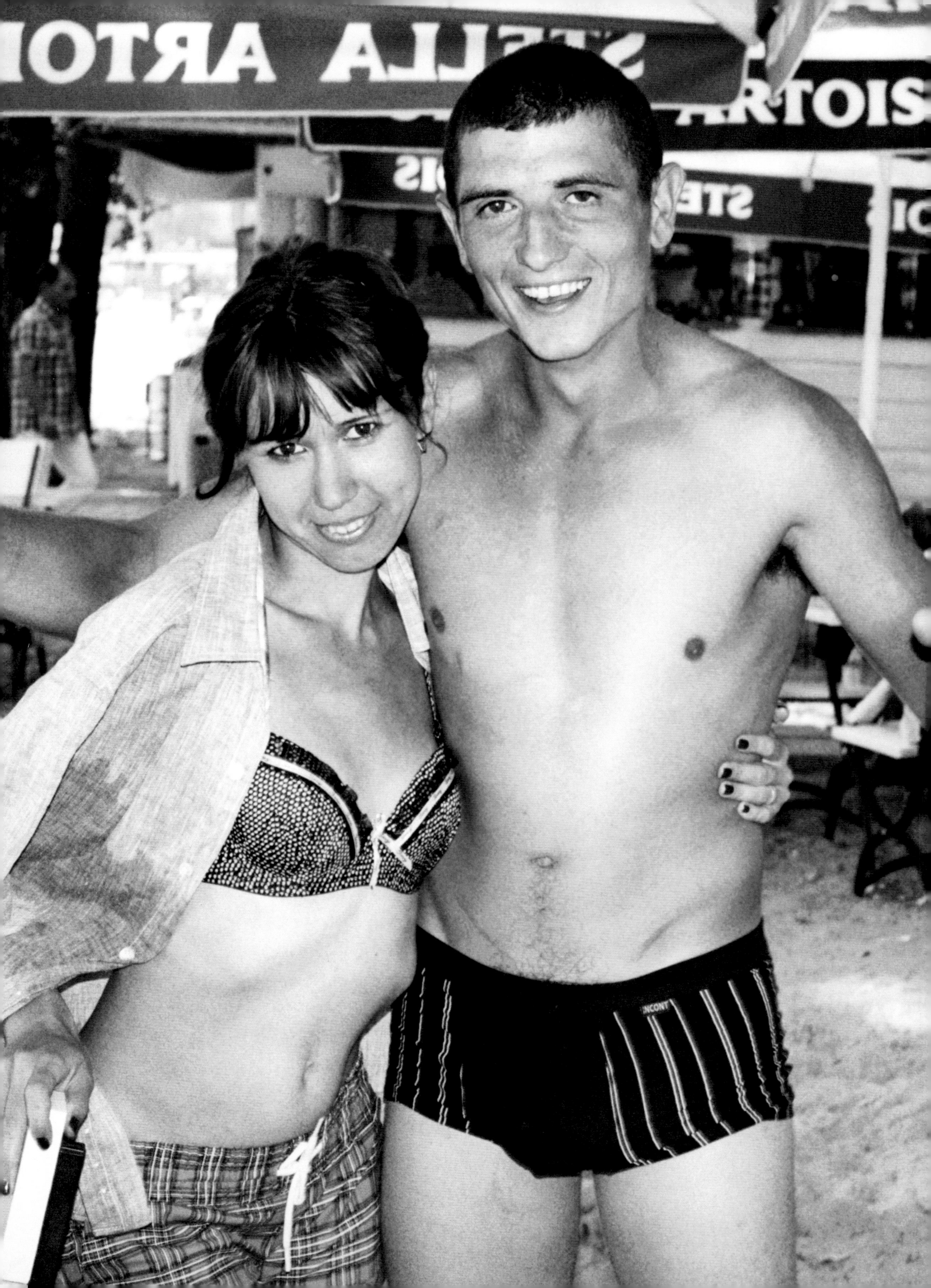
ARTOIS

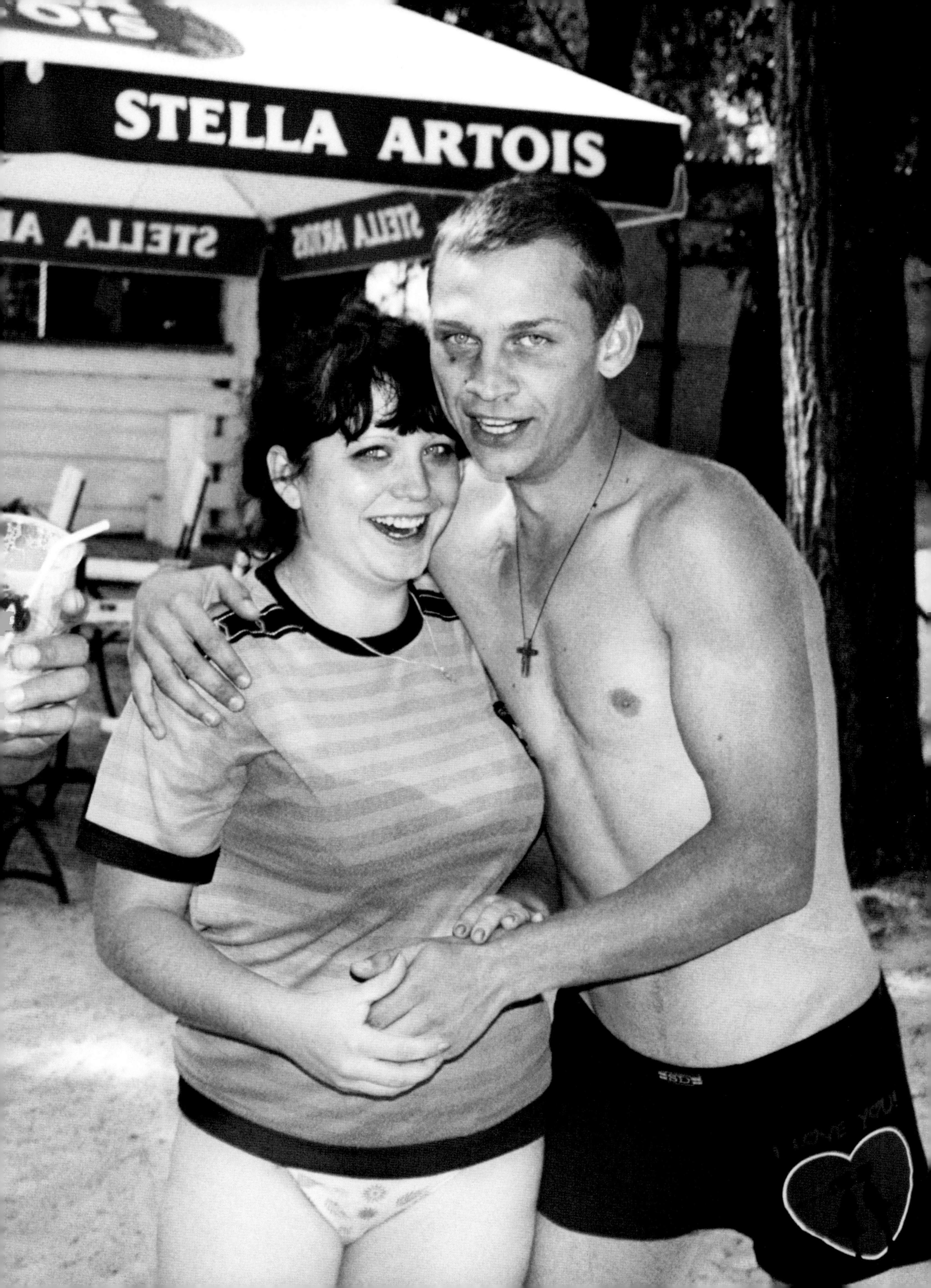
STELLA ARTOIS

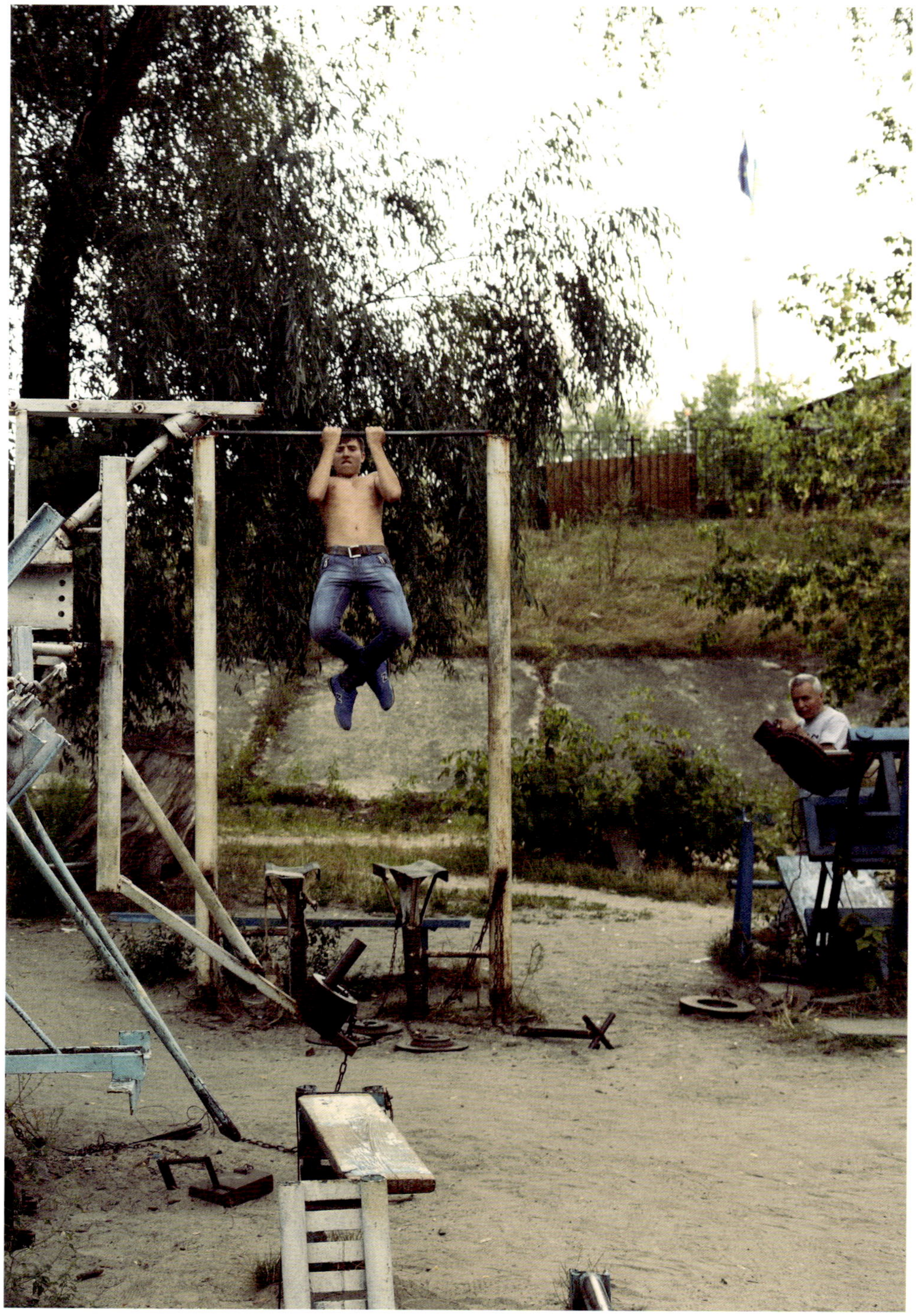

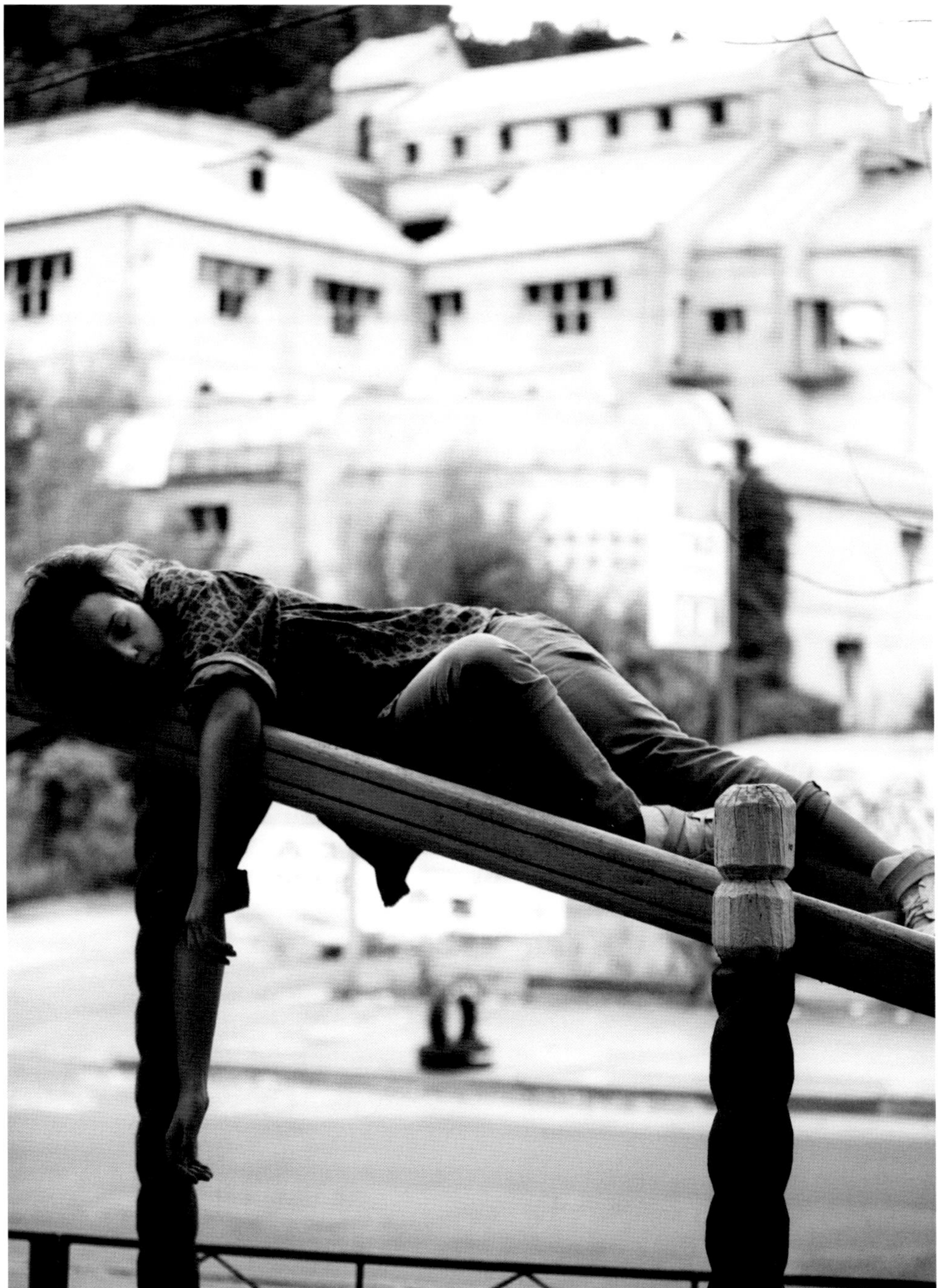

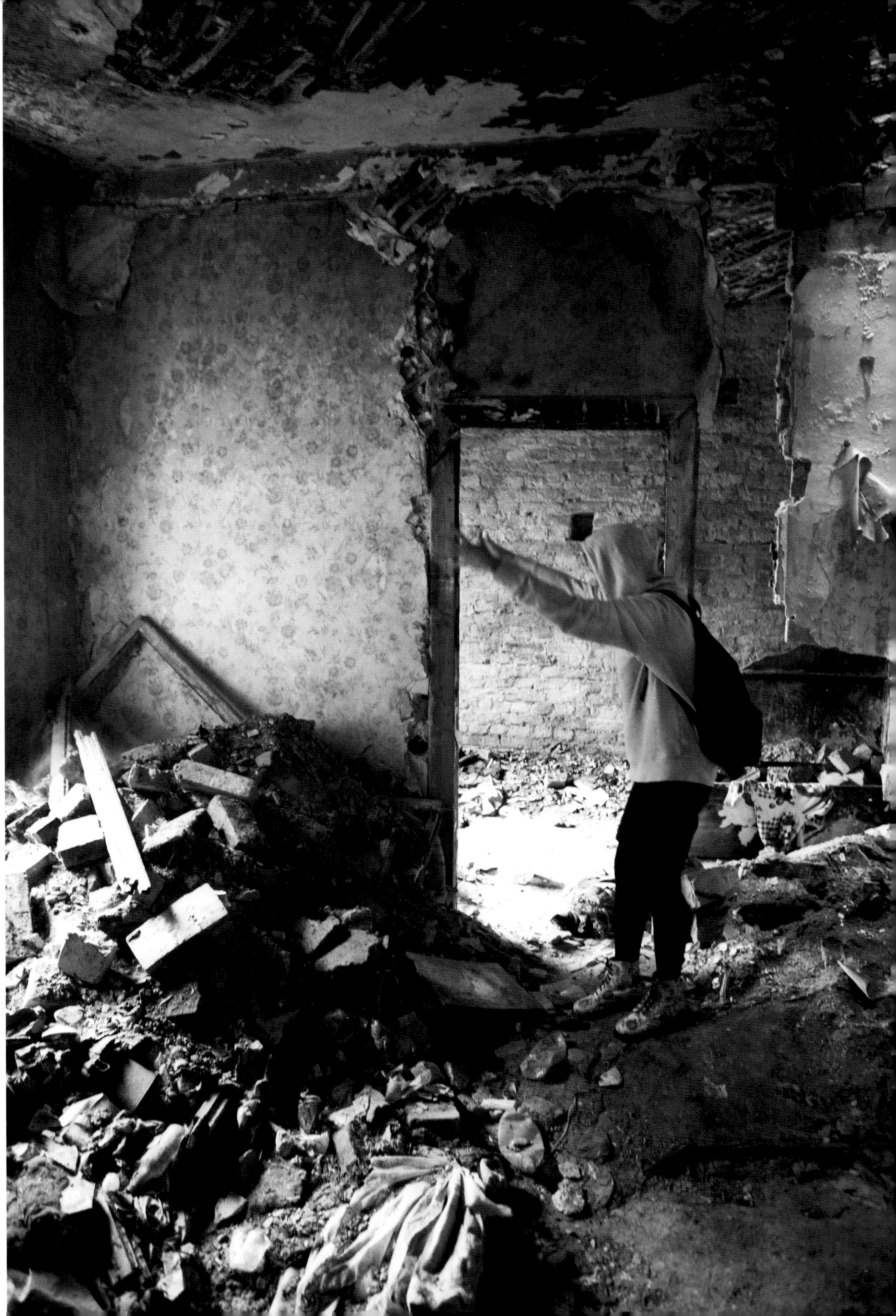

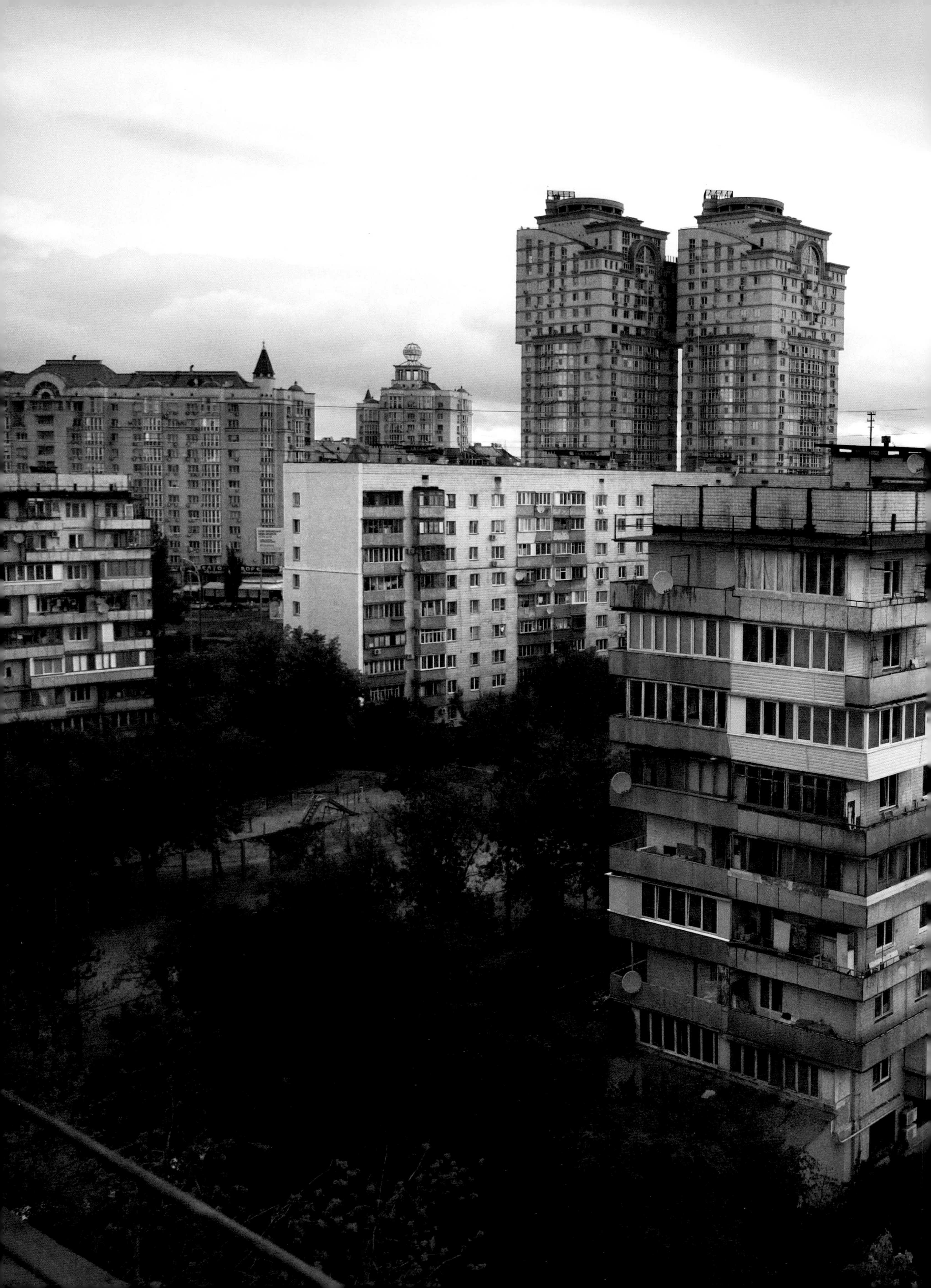

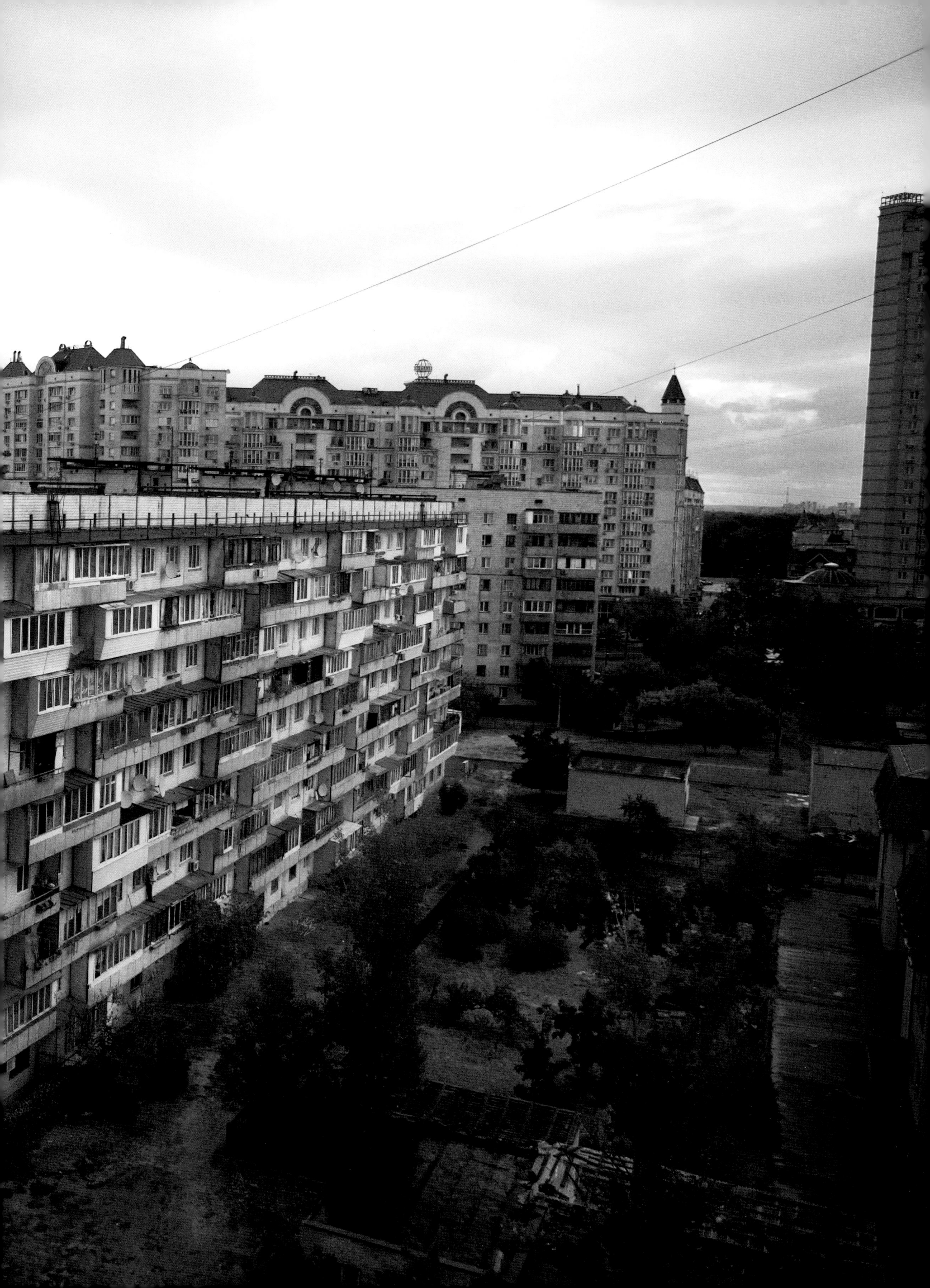

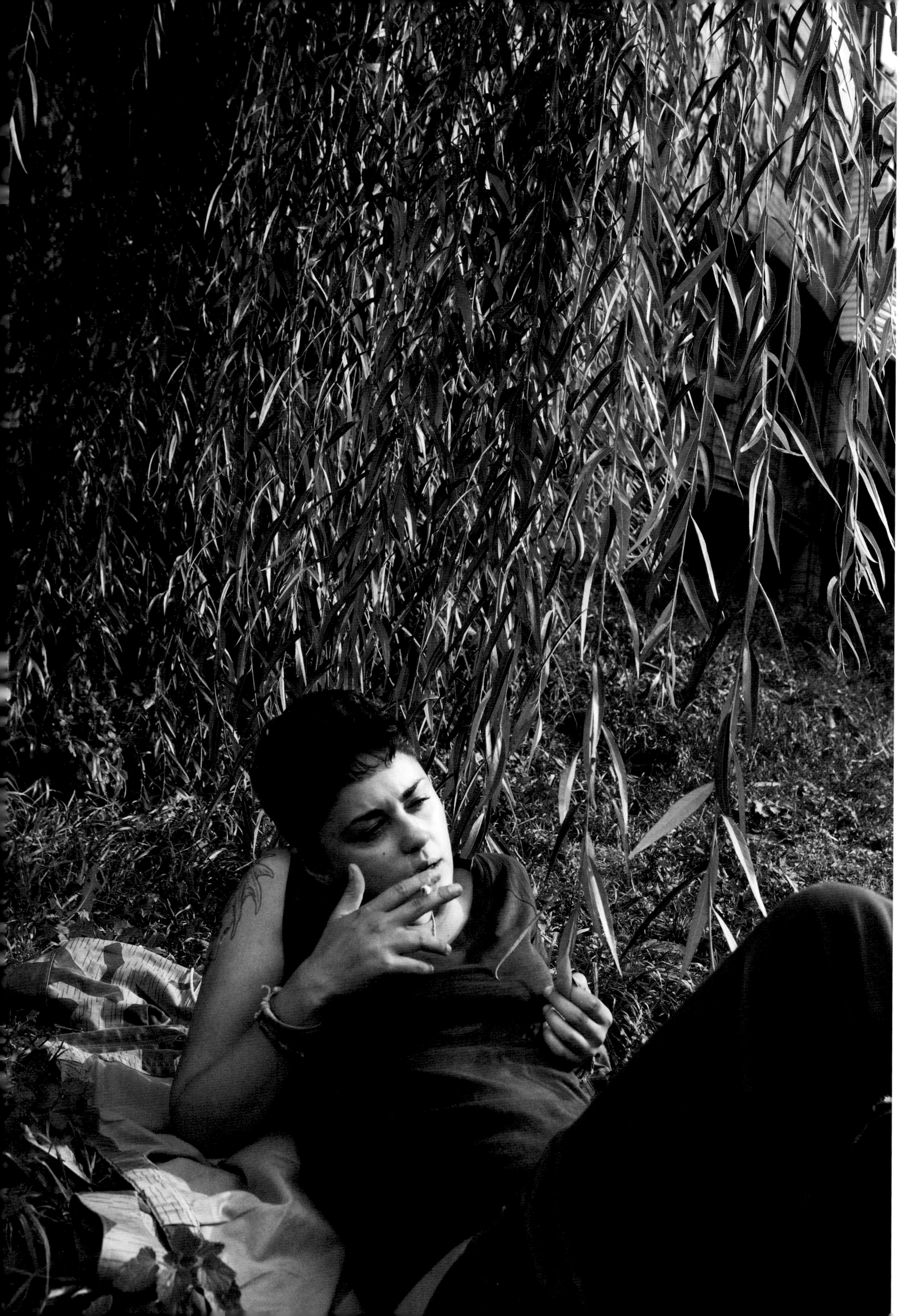

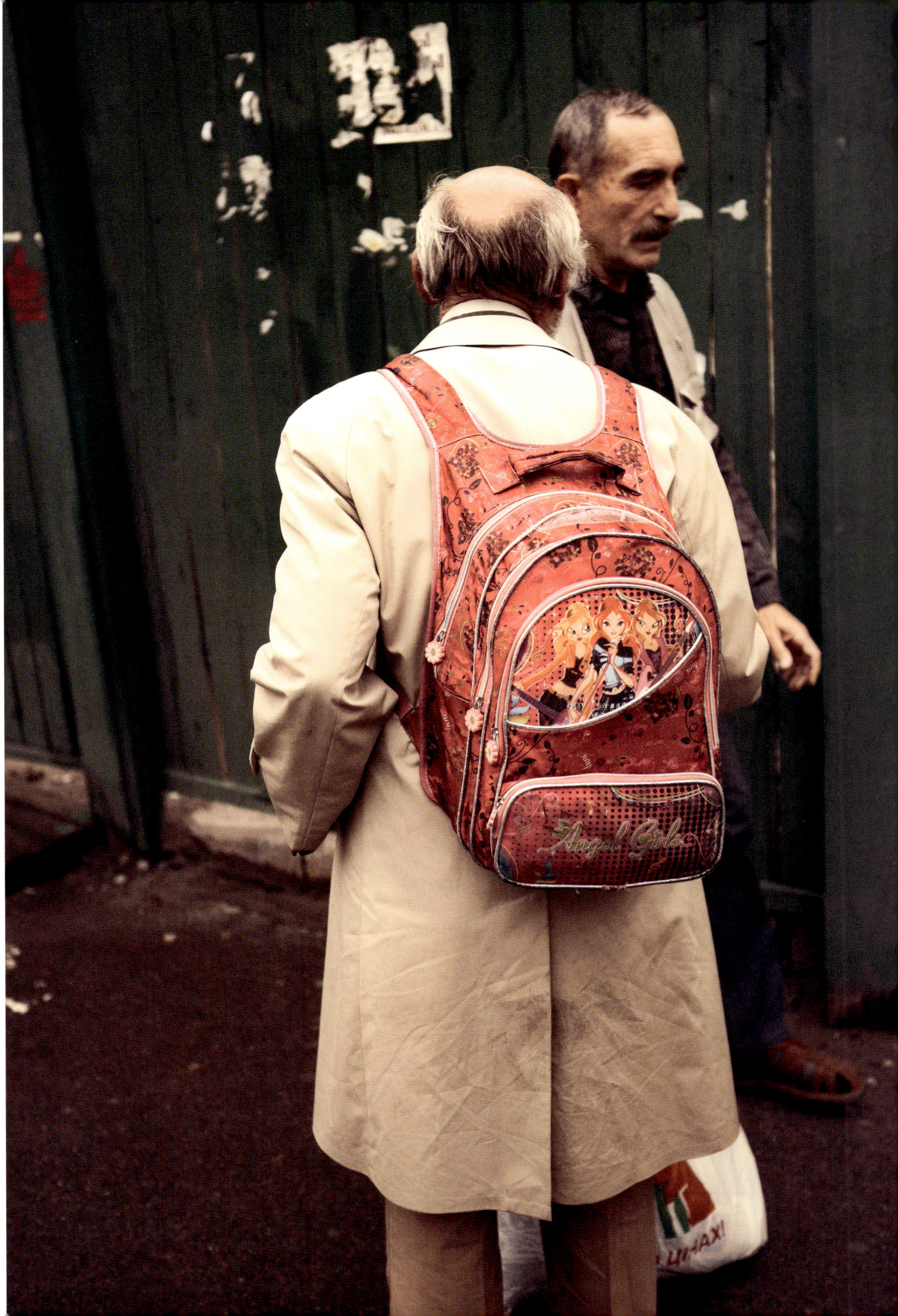
Angel Girls

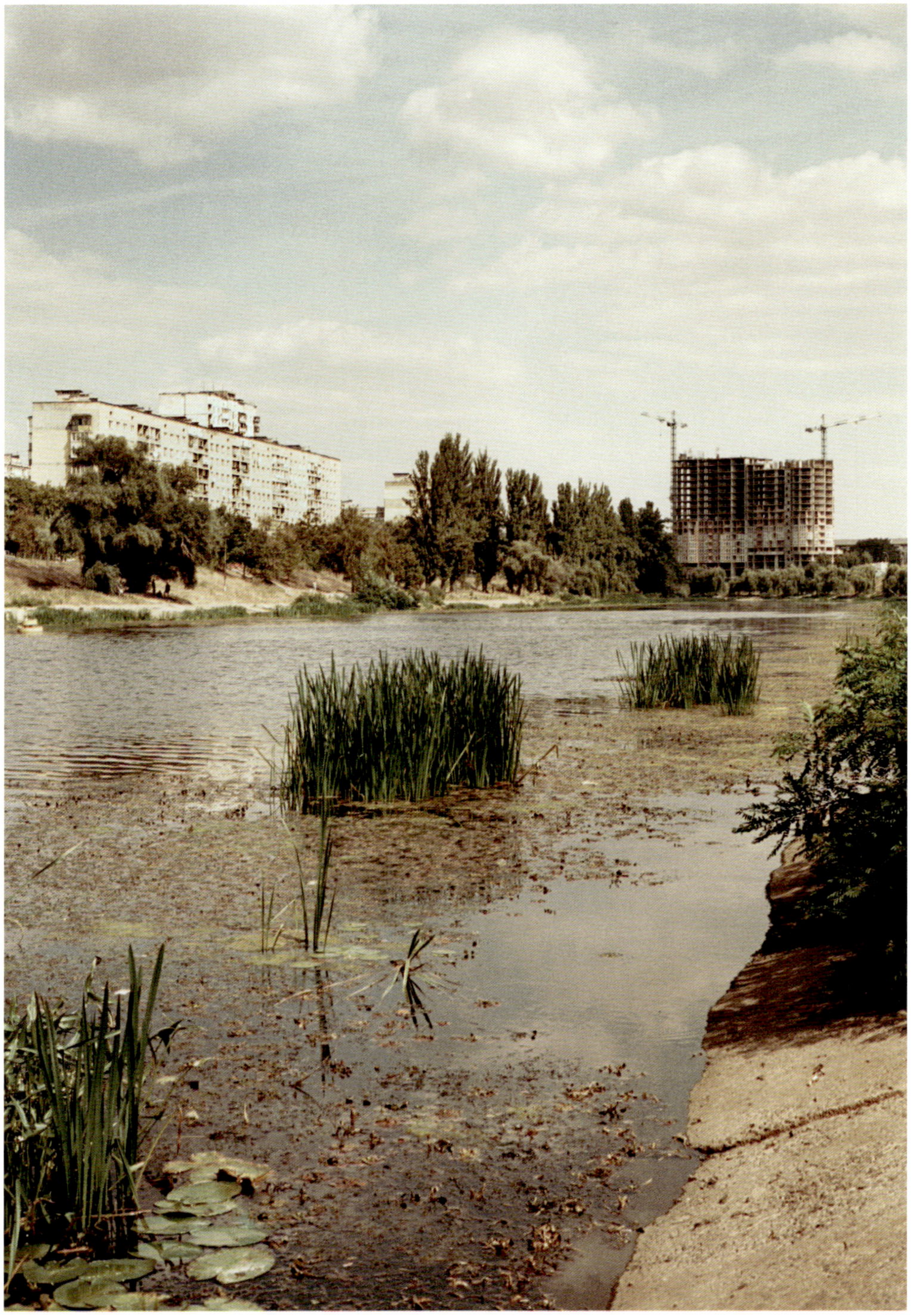

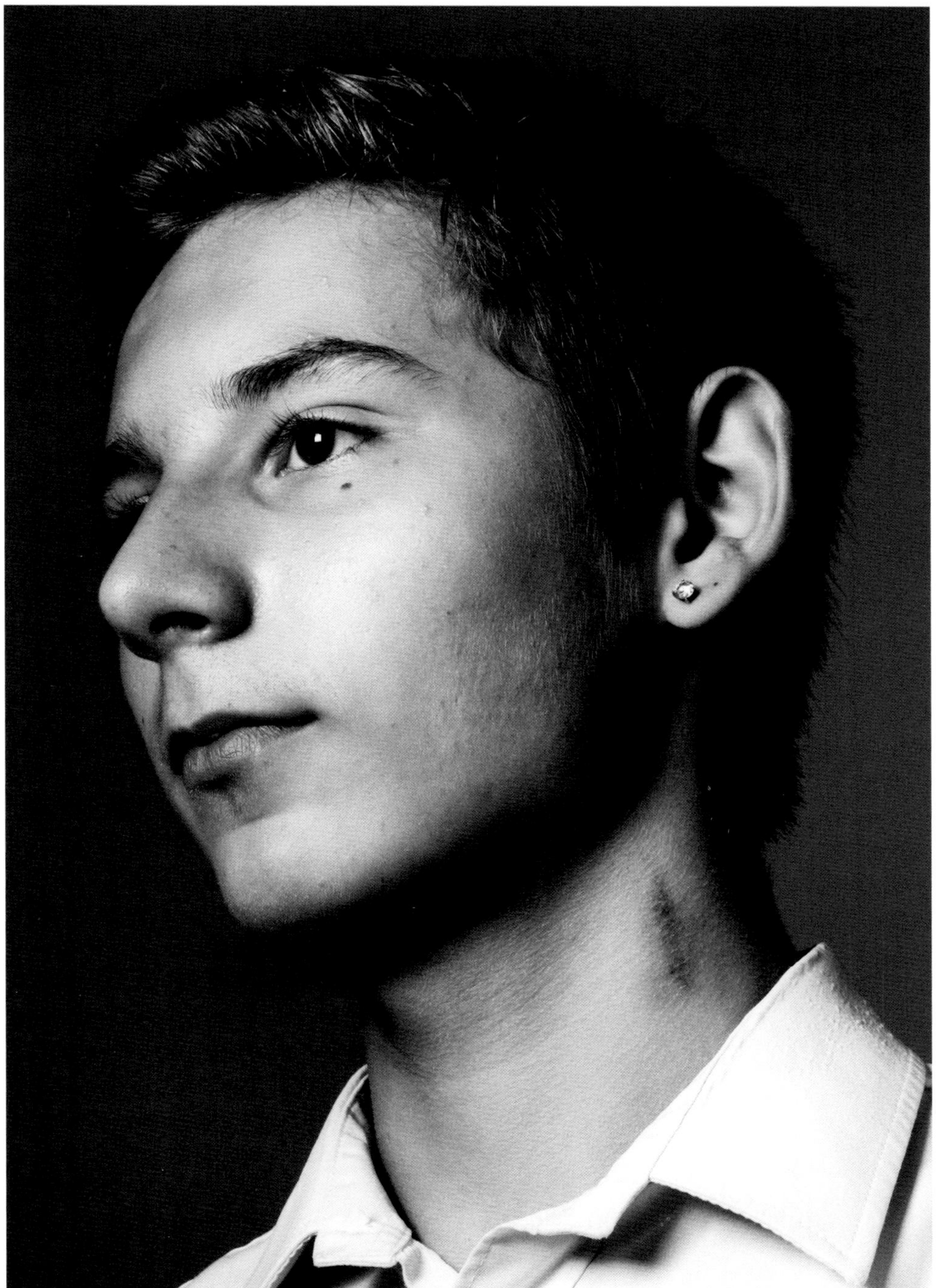

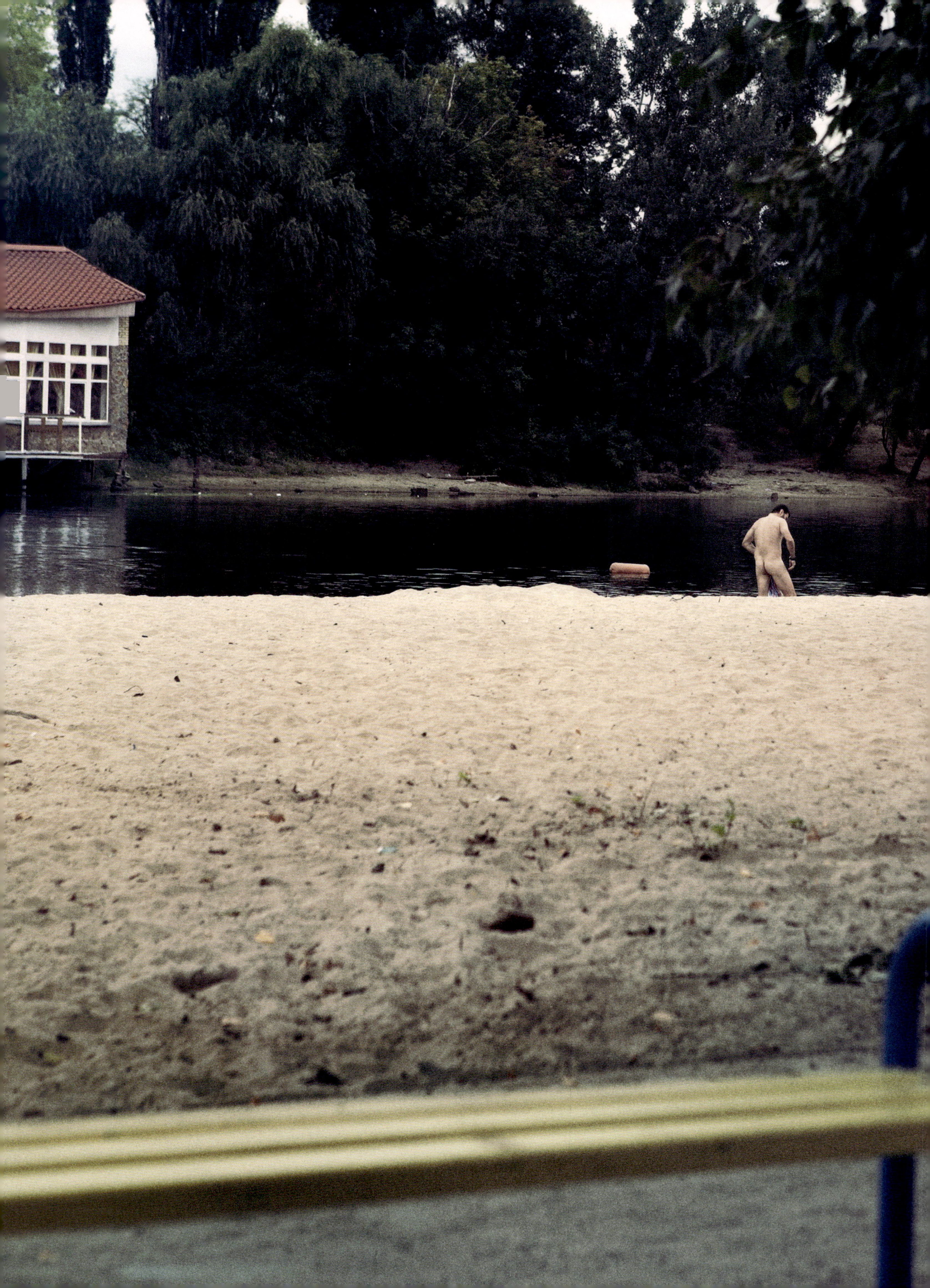

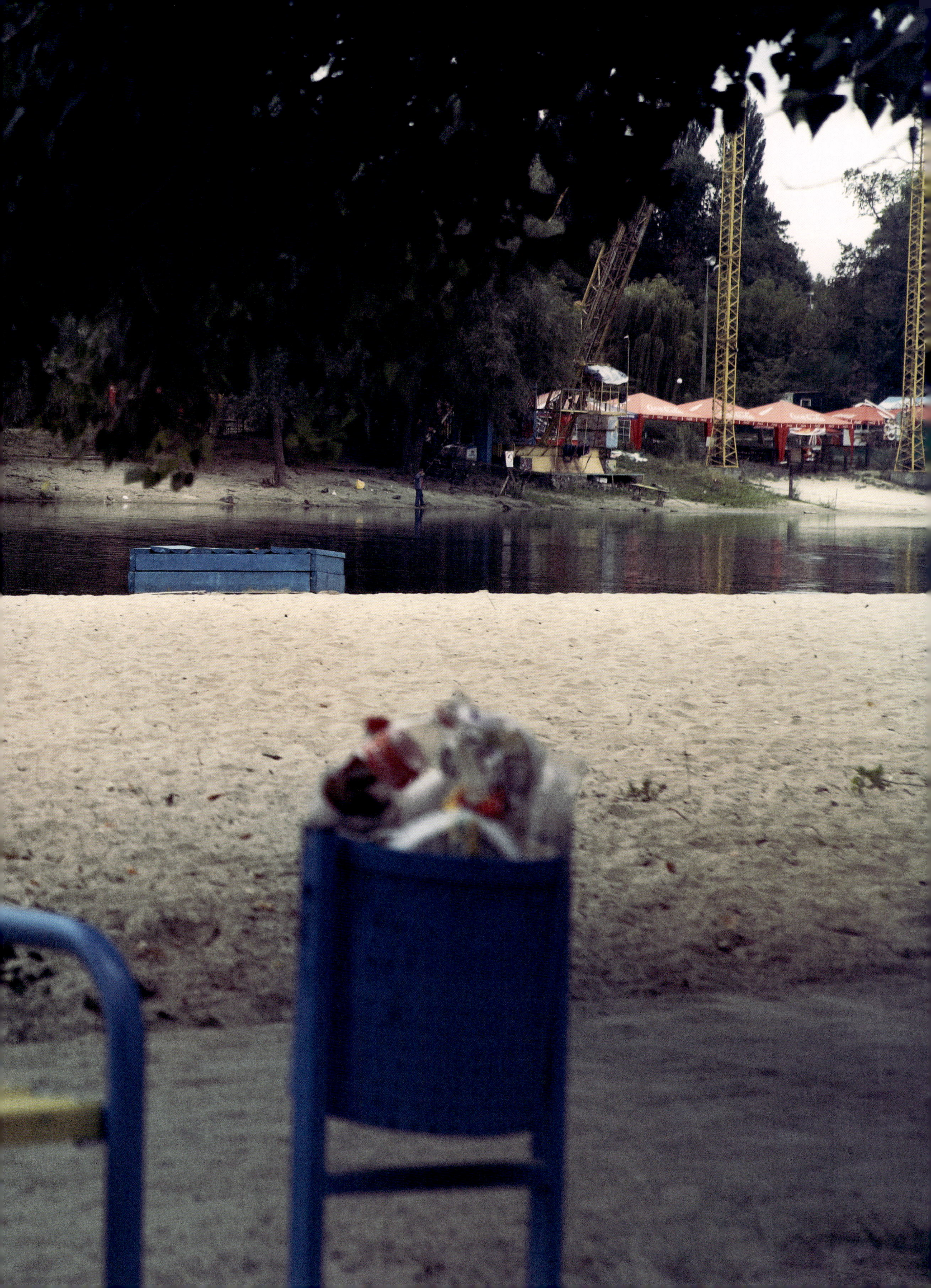

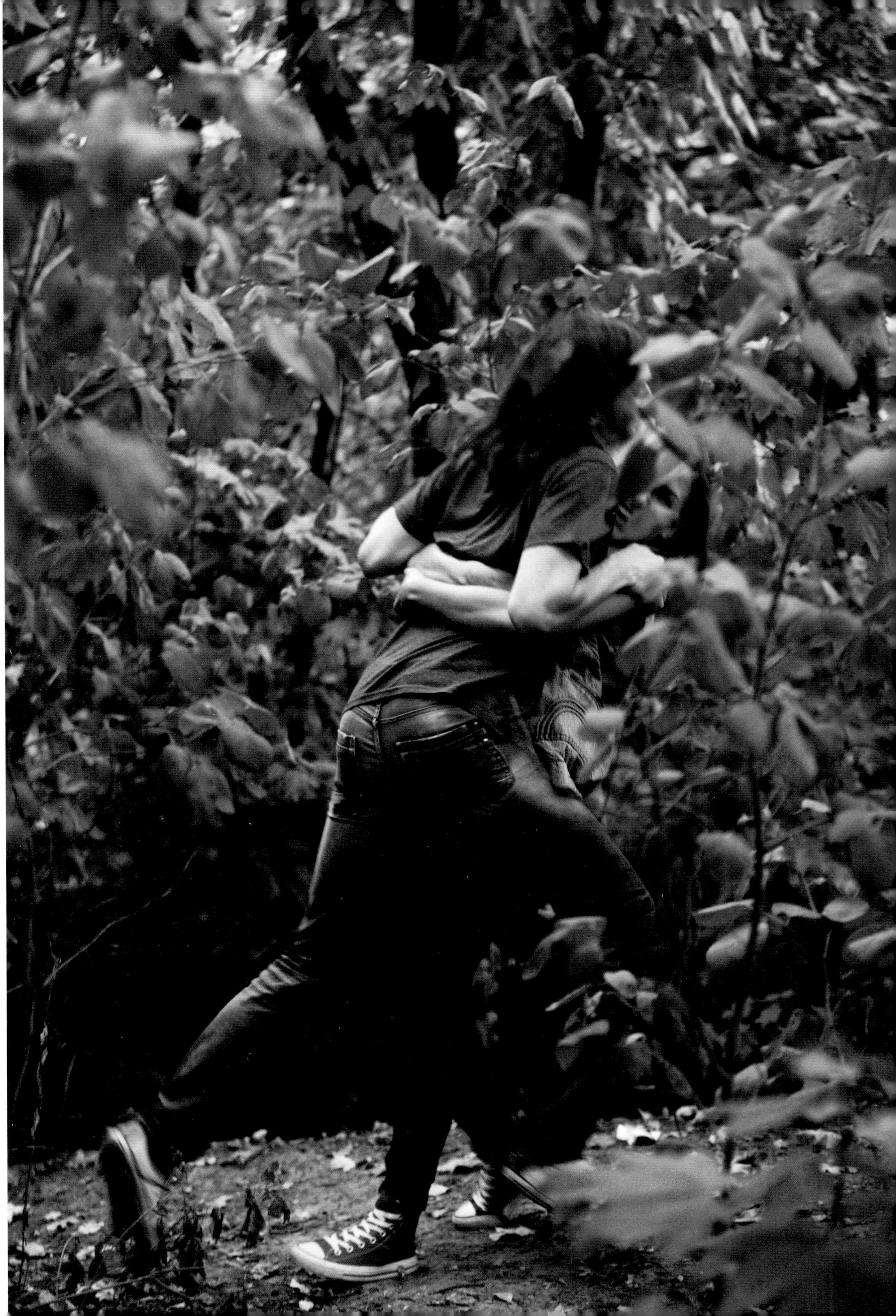

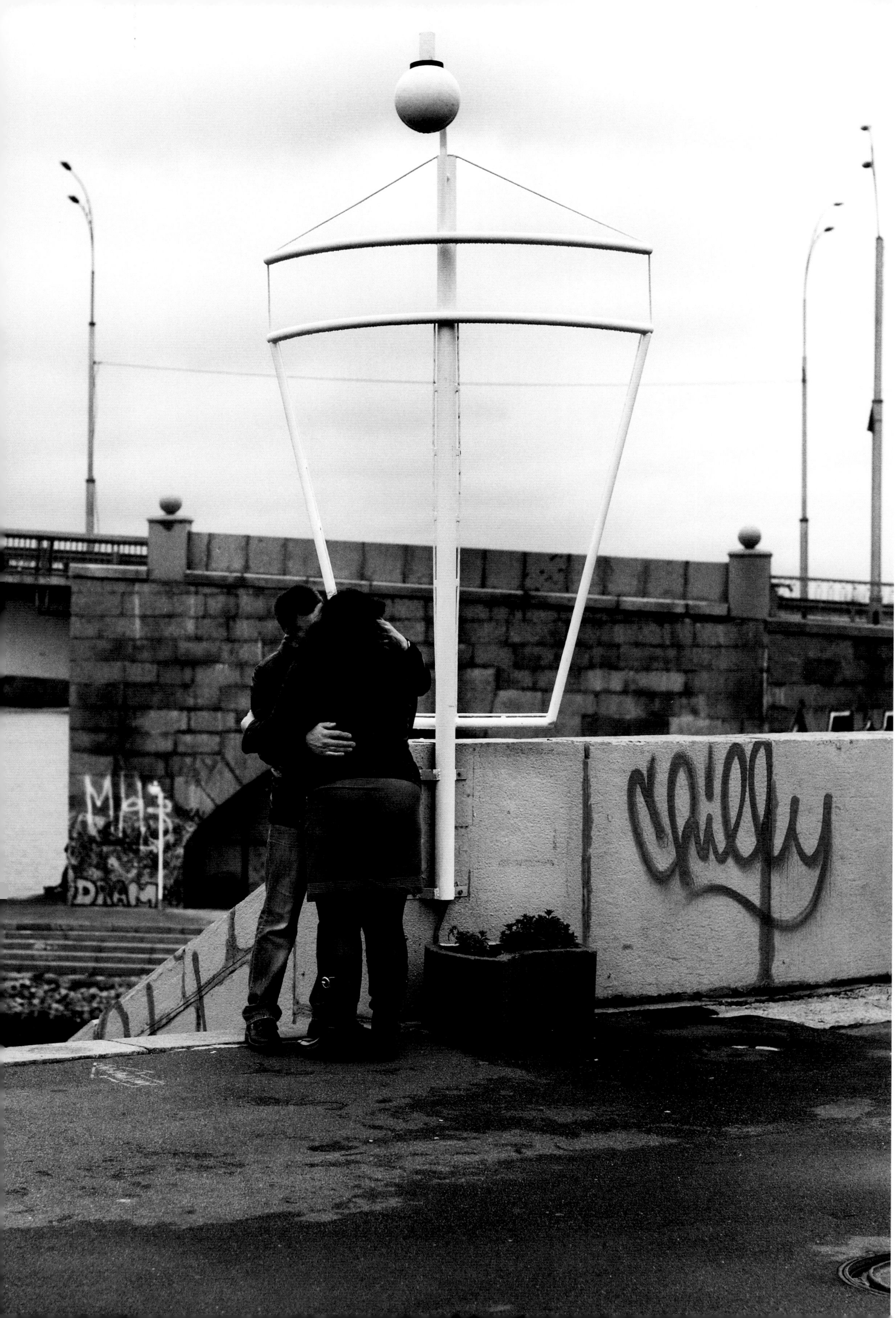

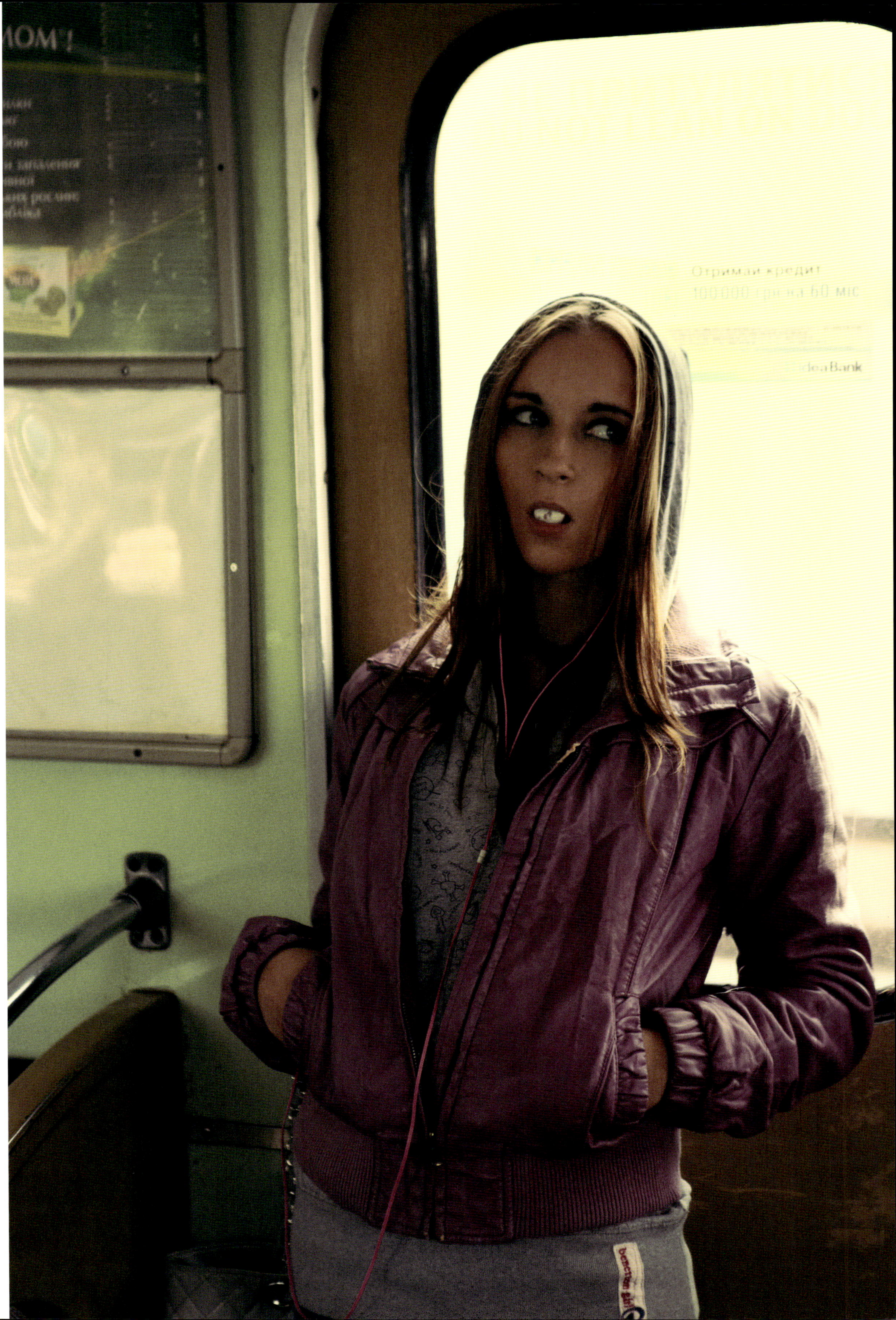
Отримай кредит
100 000 грн на 60 міс
ideaBank

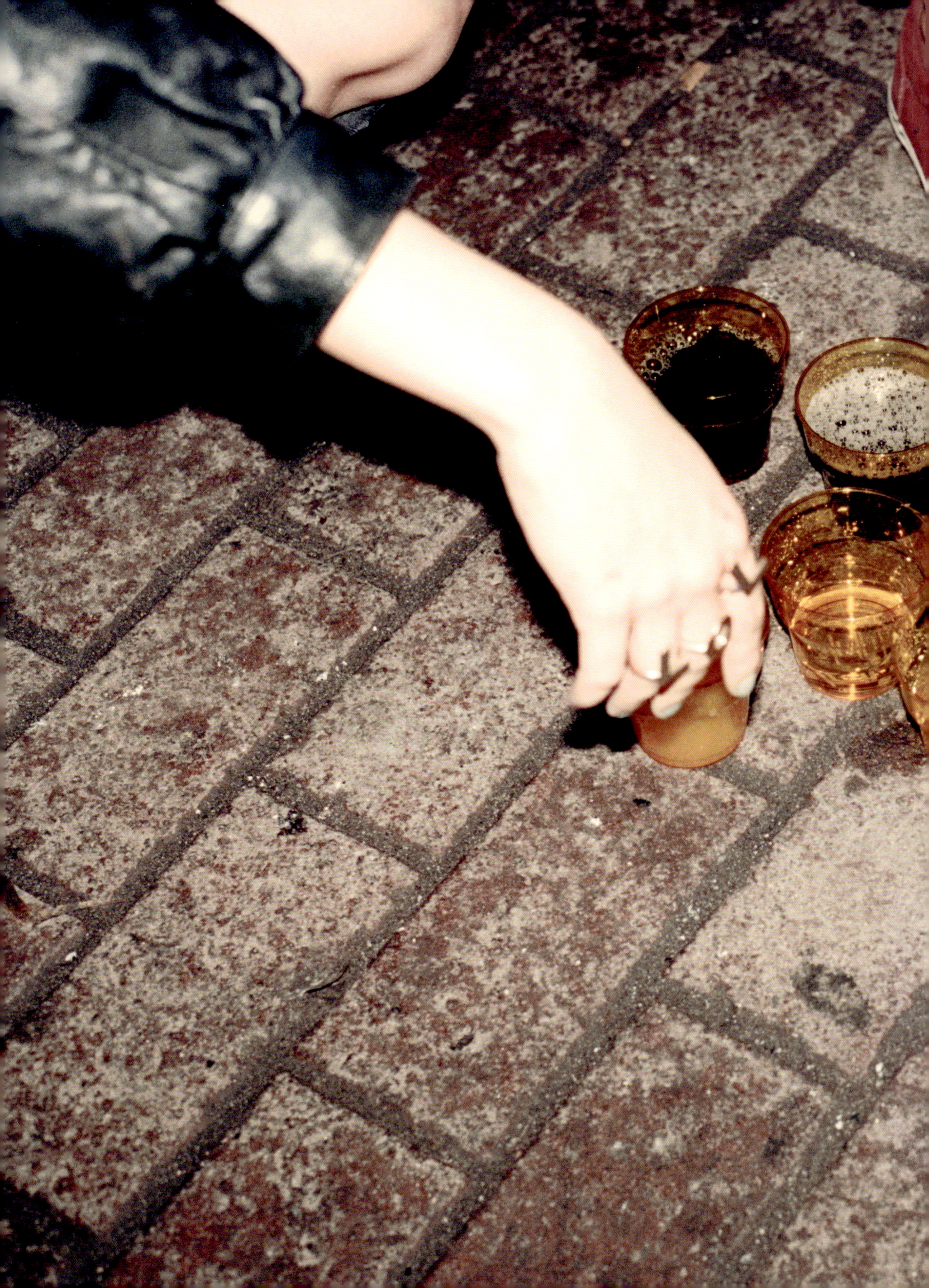

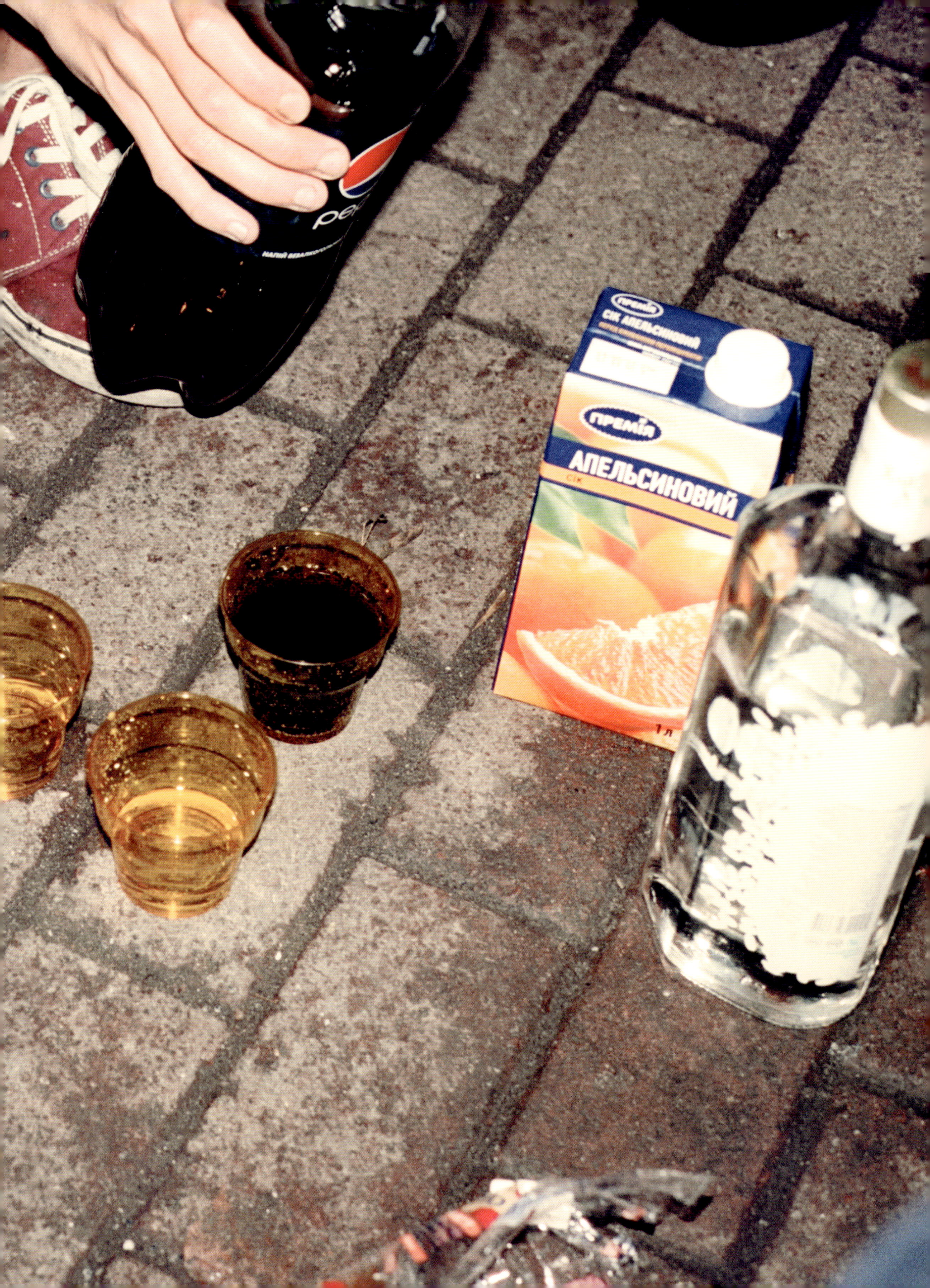
ПРЕМІЯ
СІК АПЕЛЬСИНОВИЙ
ПРЕМІЯ
АПЕЛЬСИНОВИЙ
сік
1 л

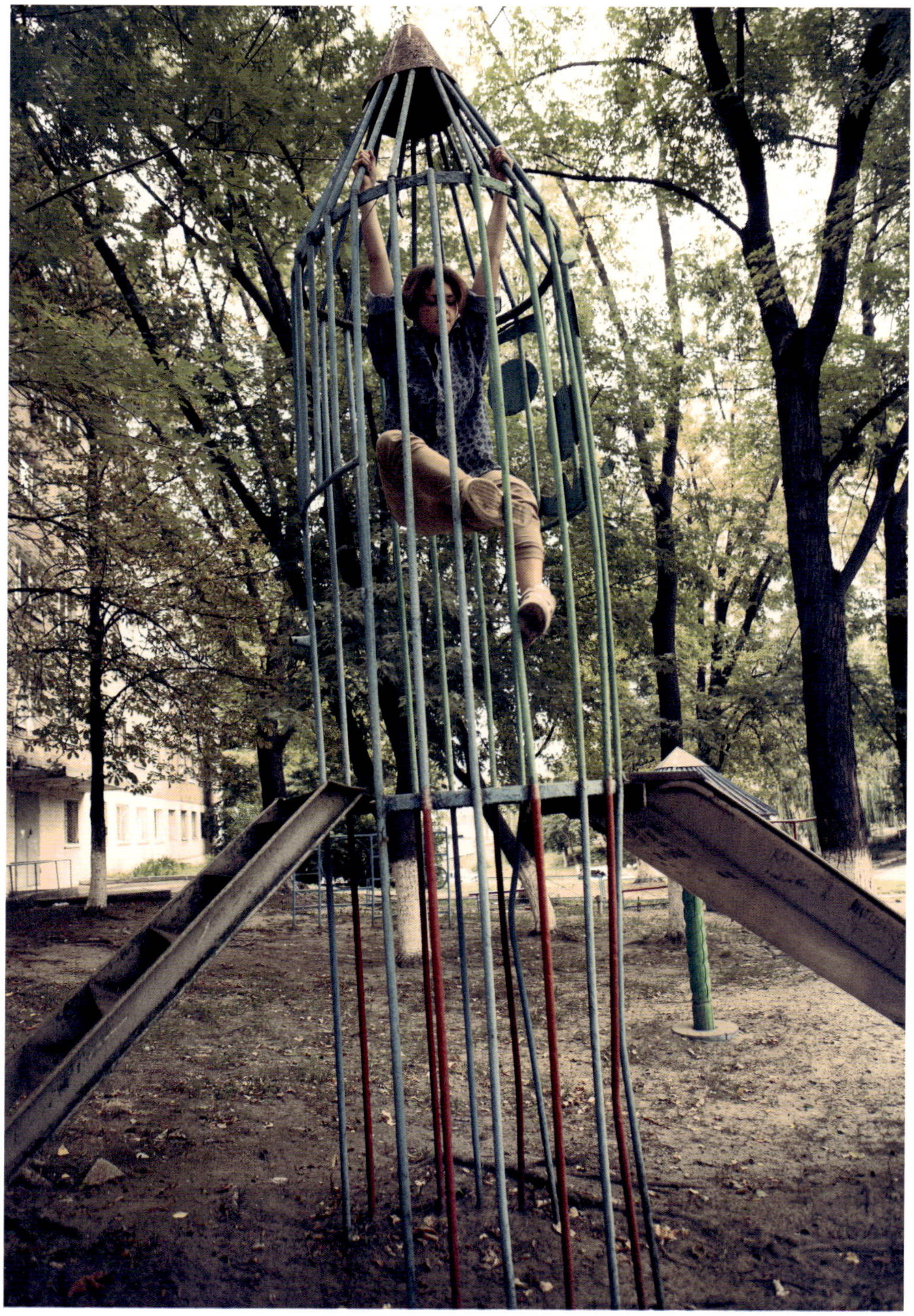

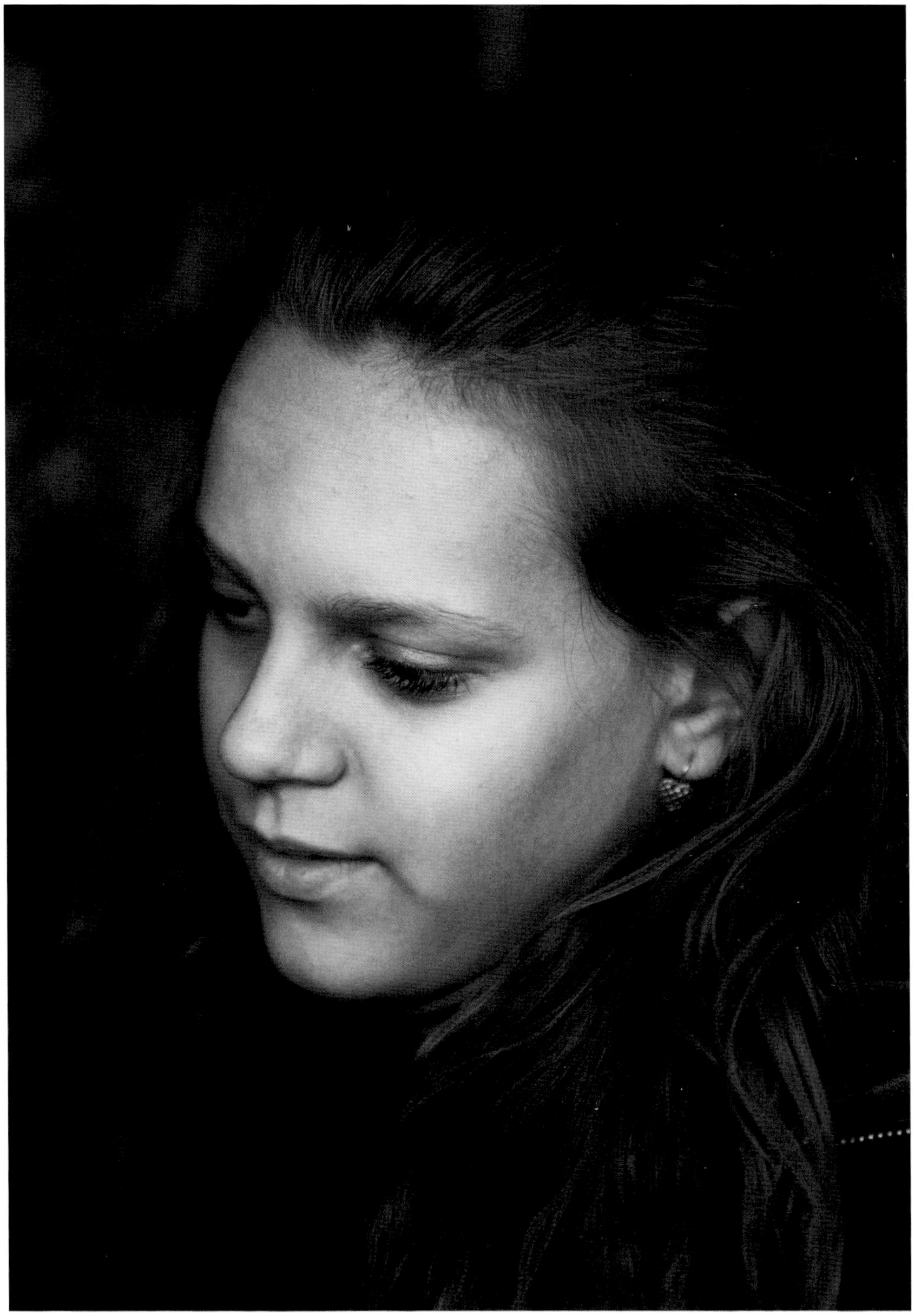

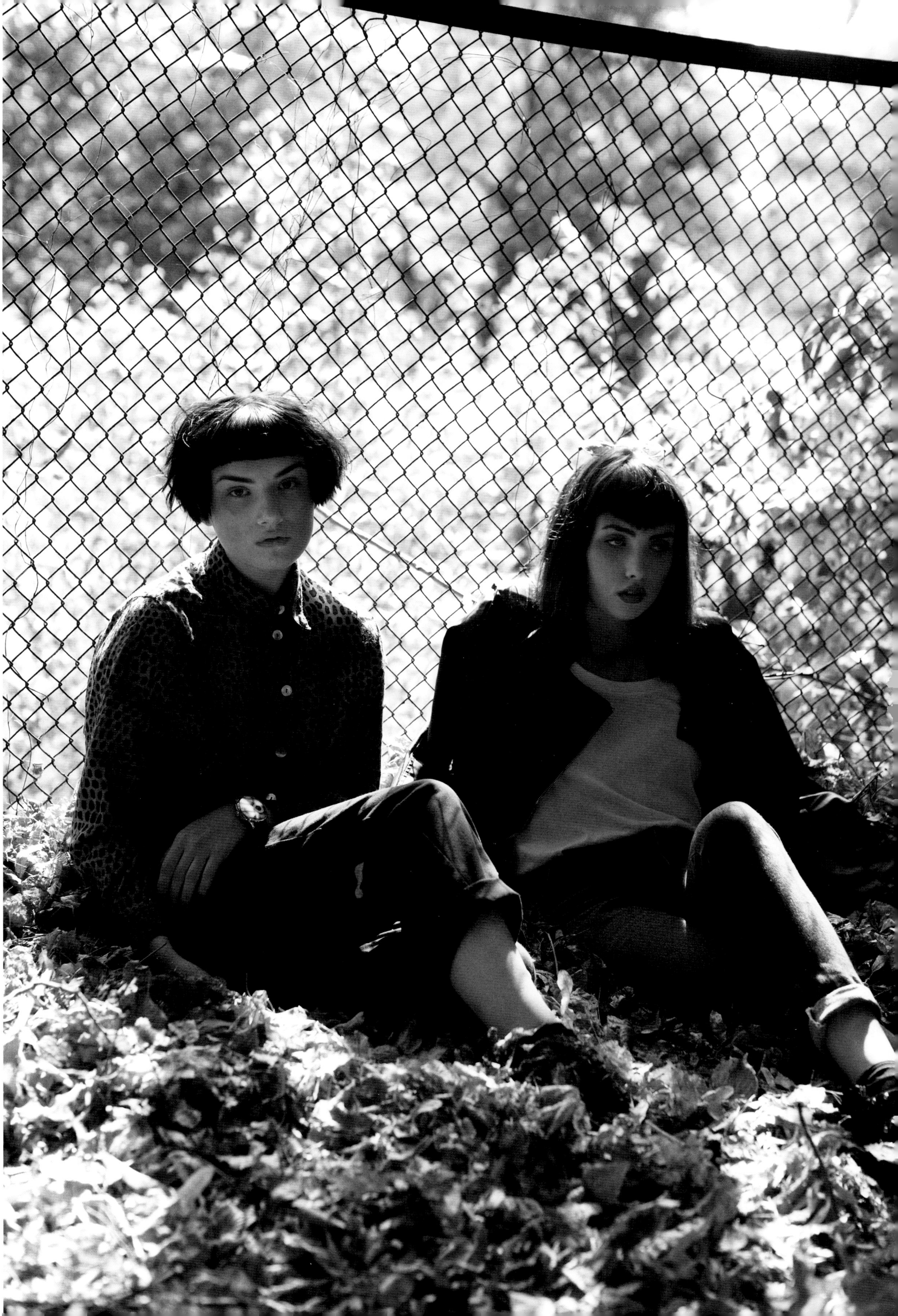

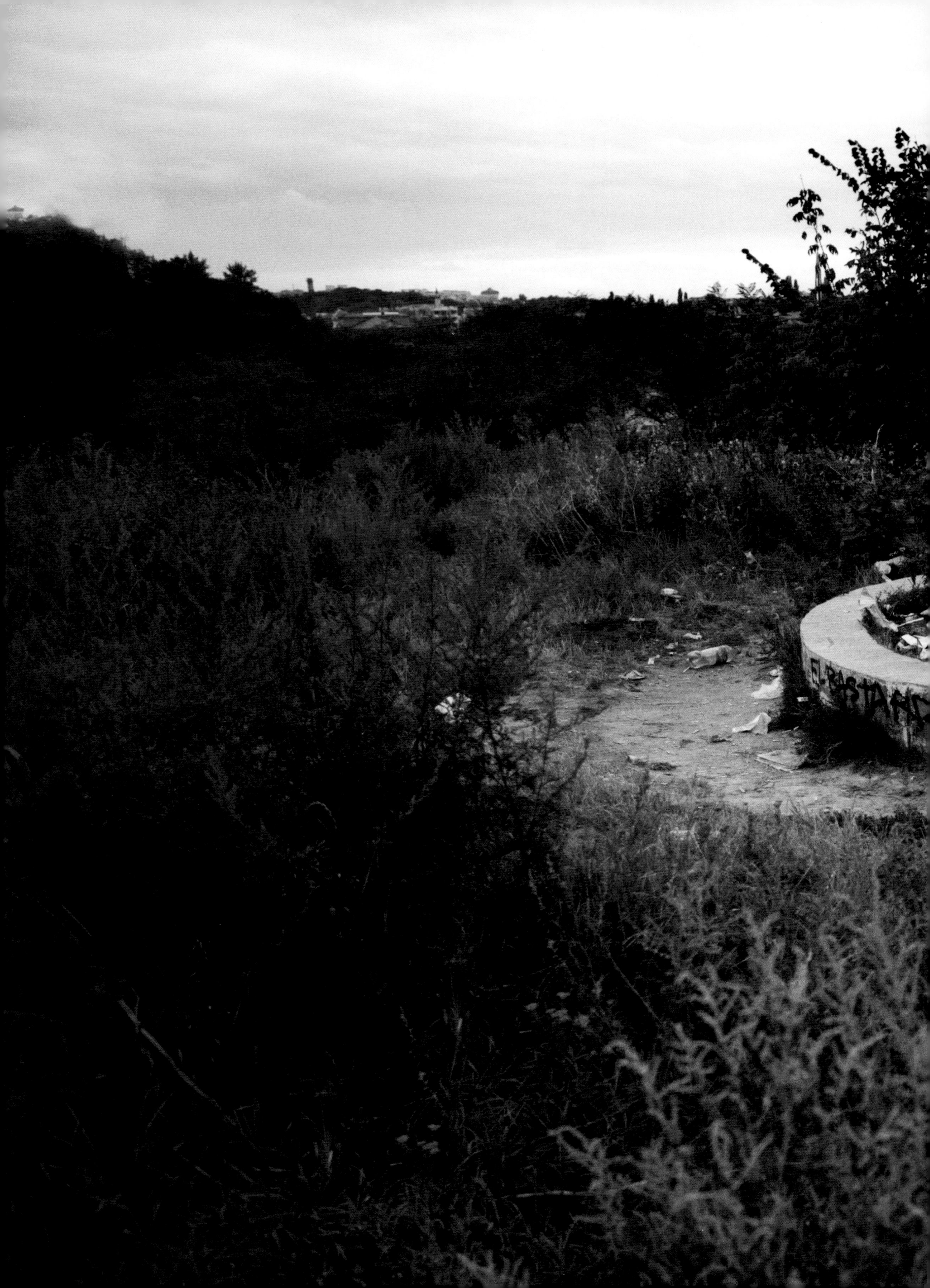

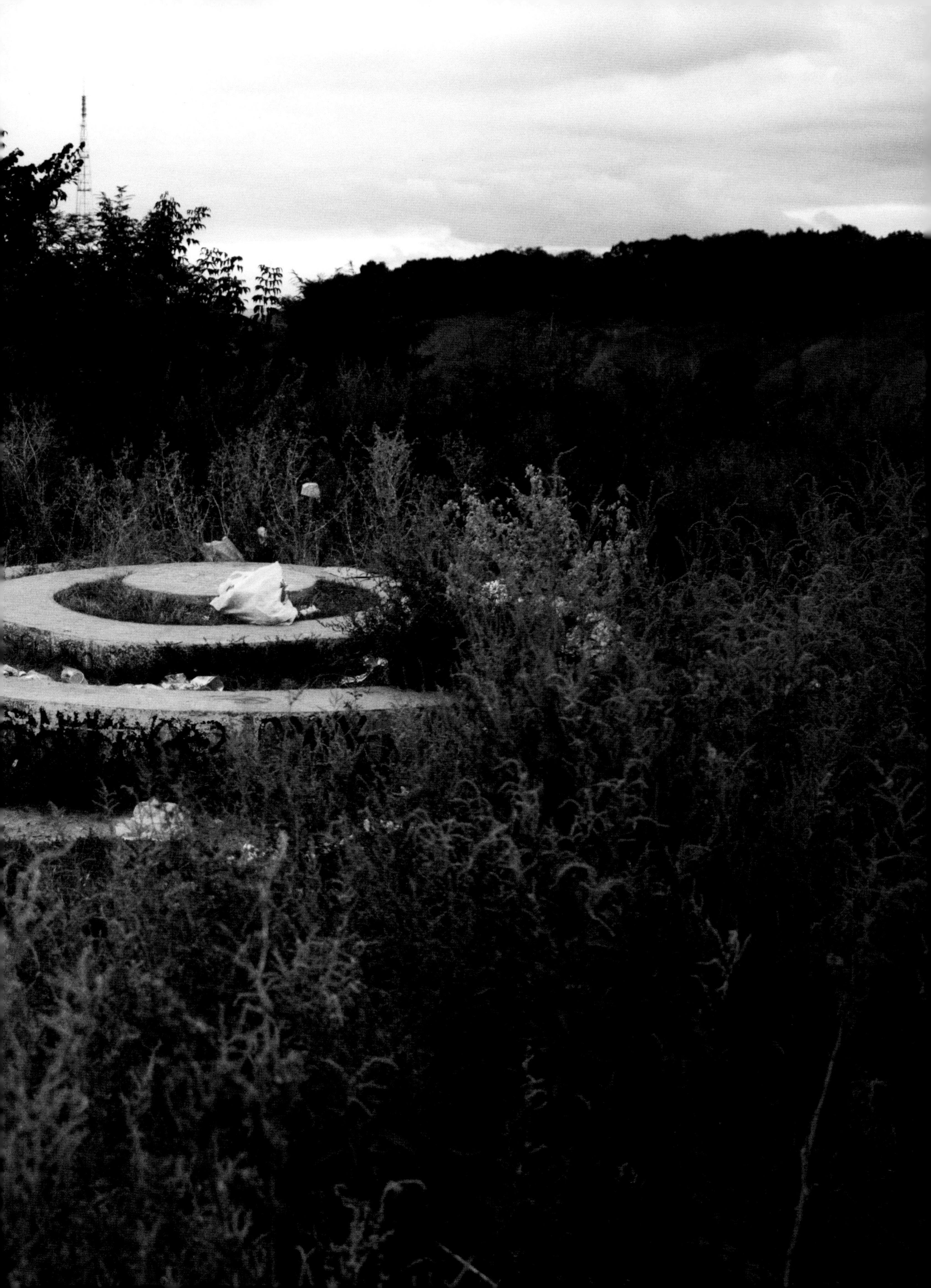

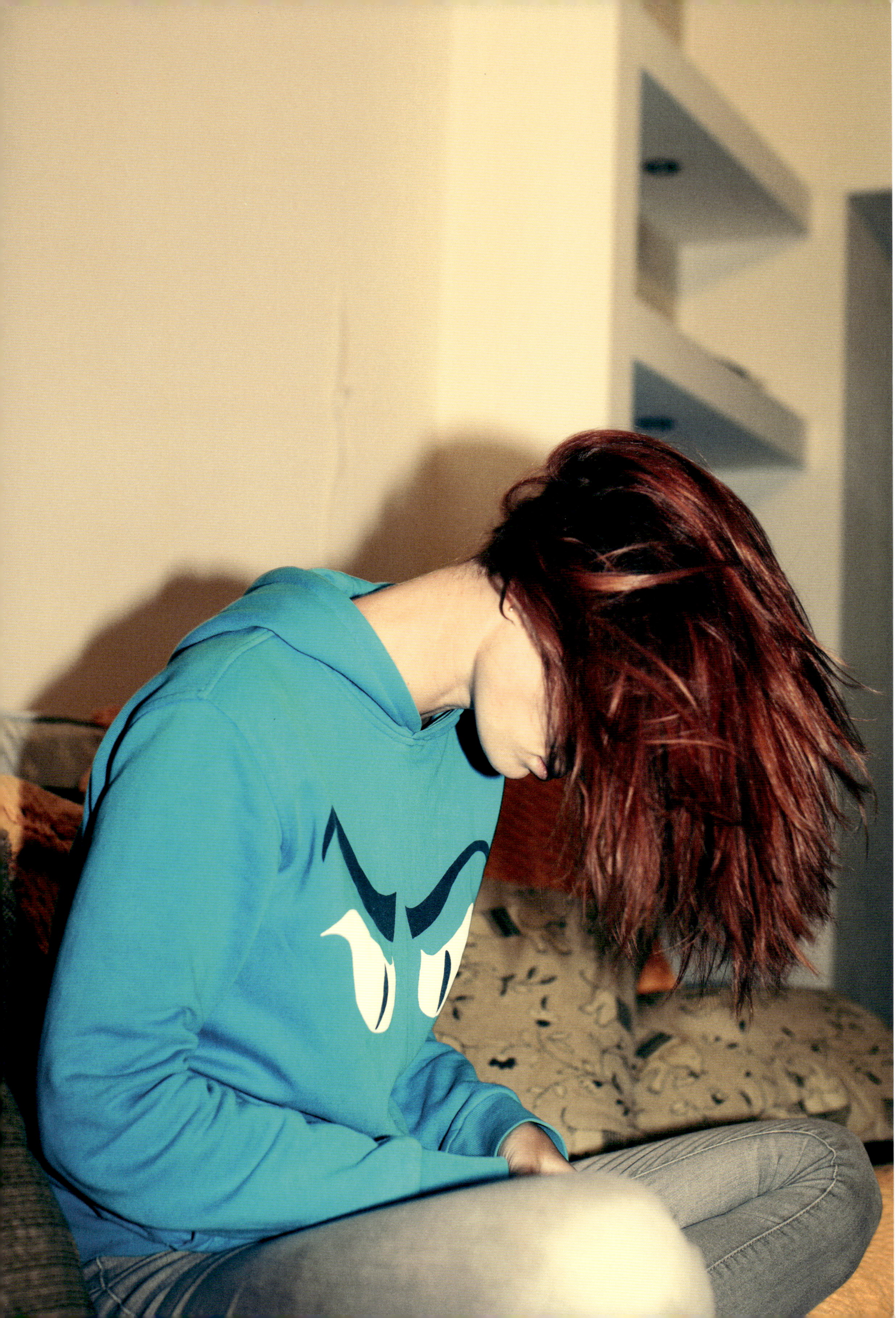

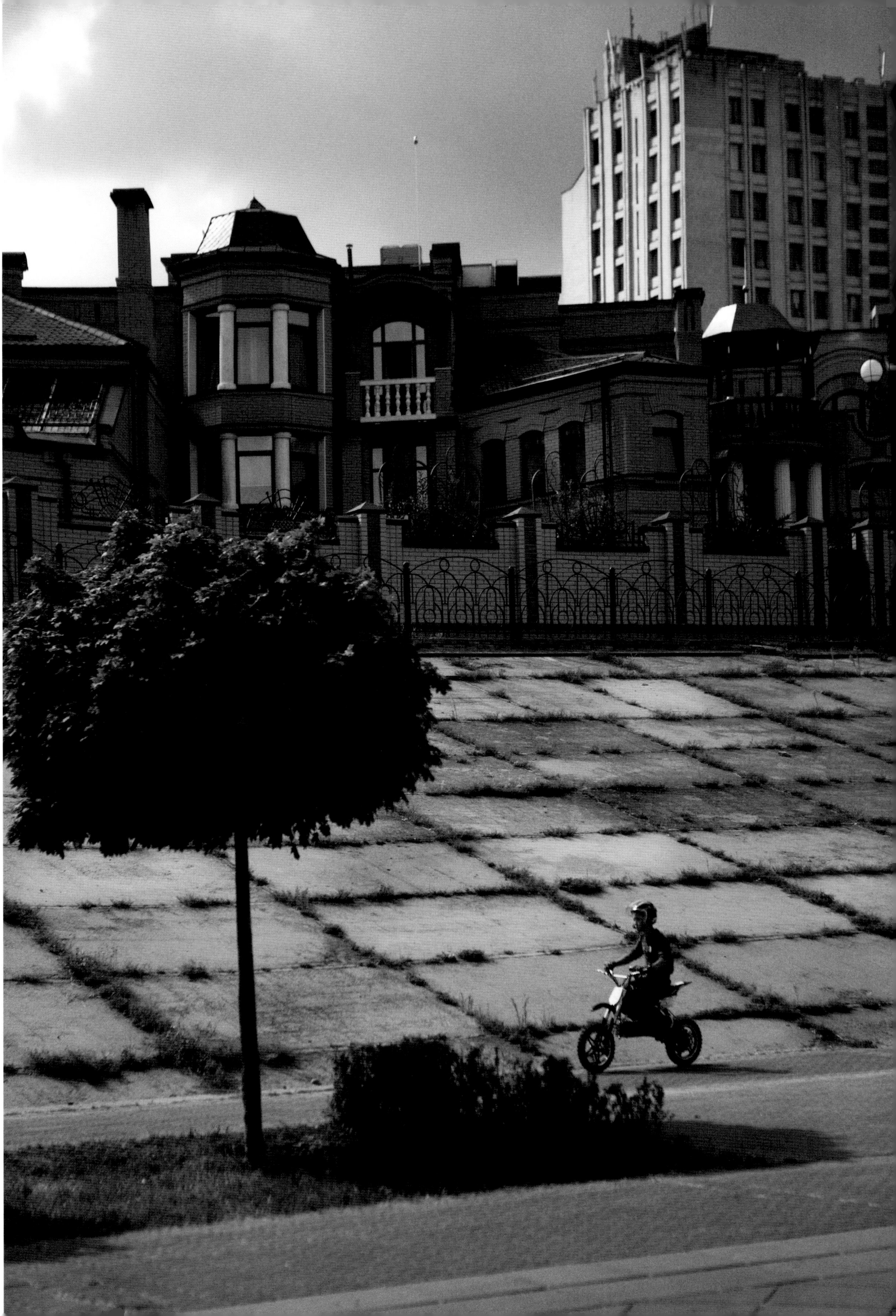

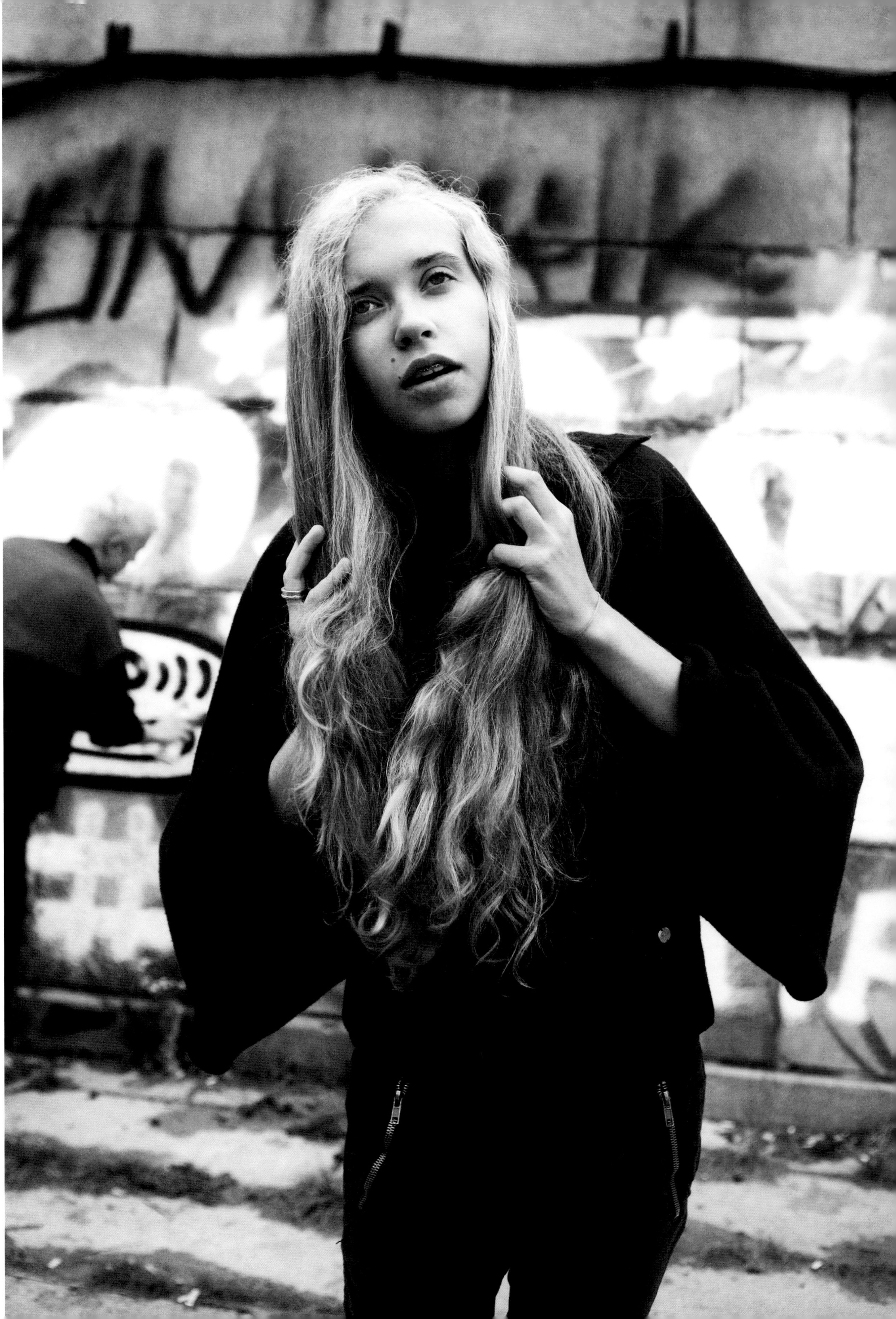

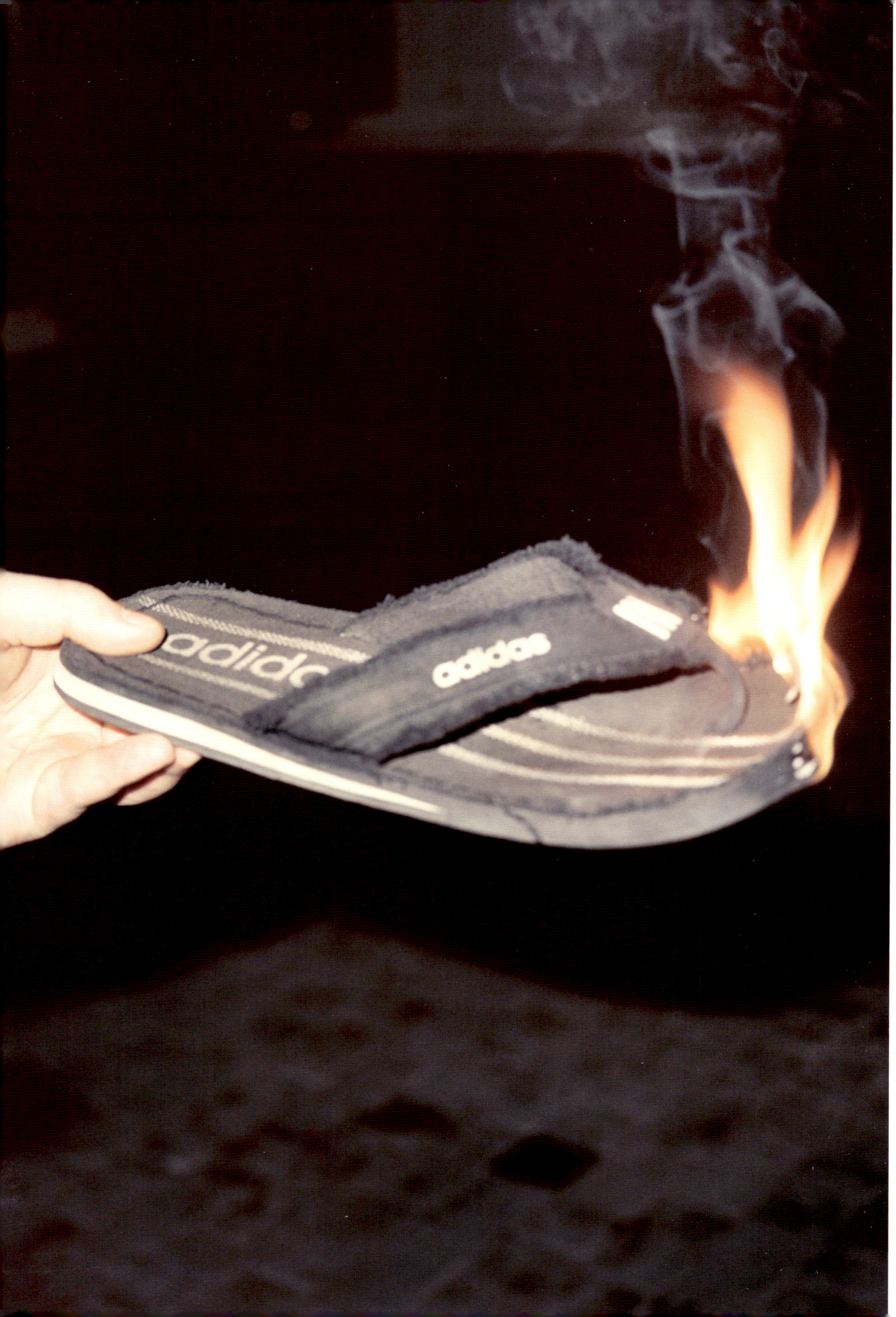
adidas

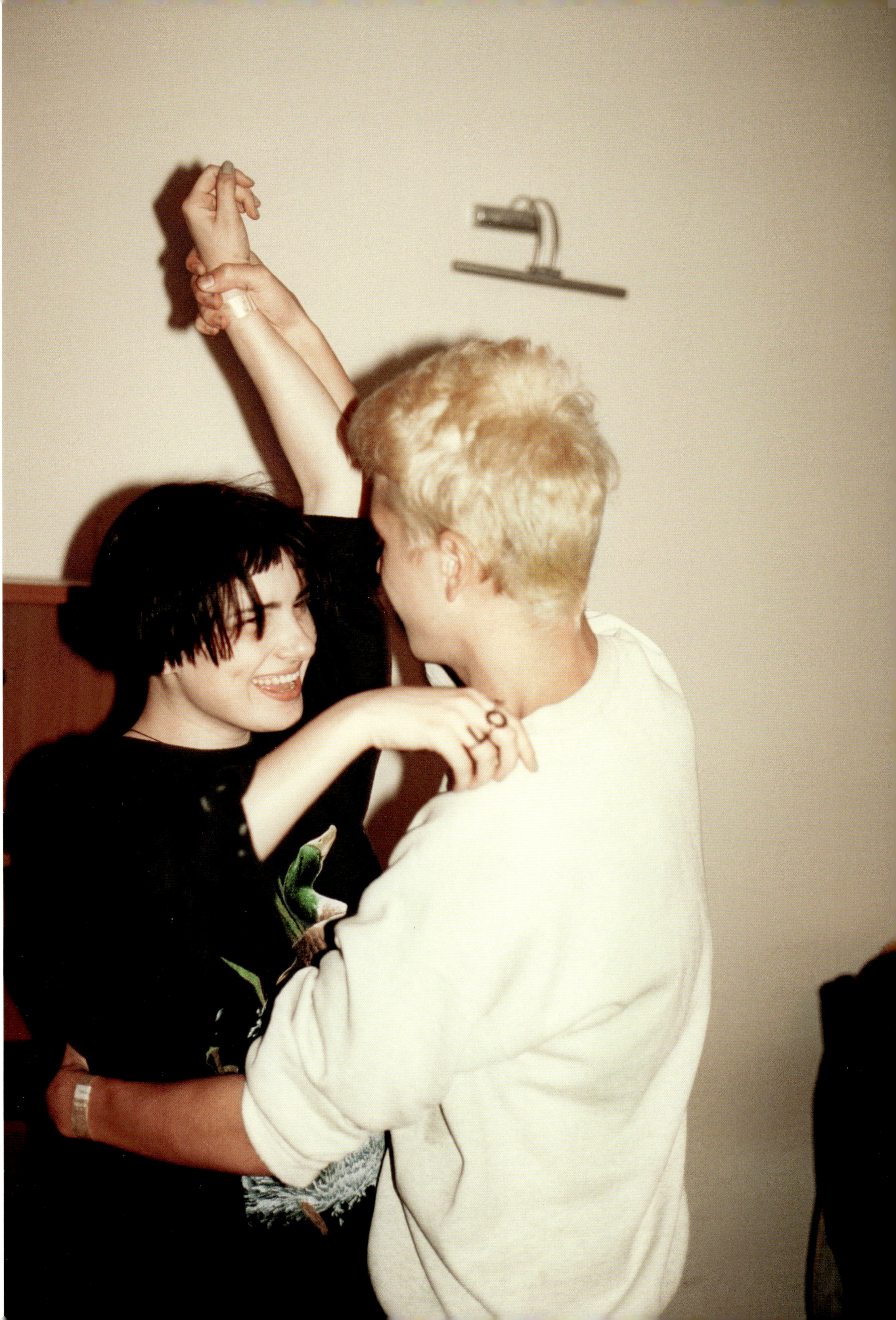

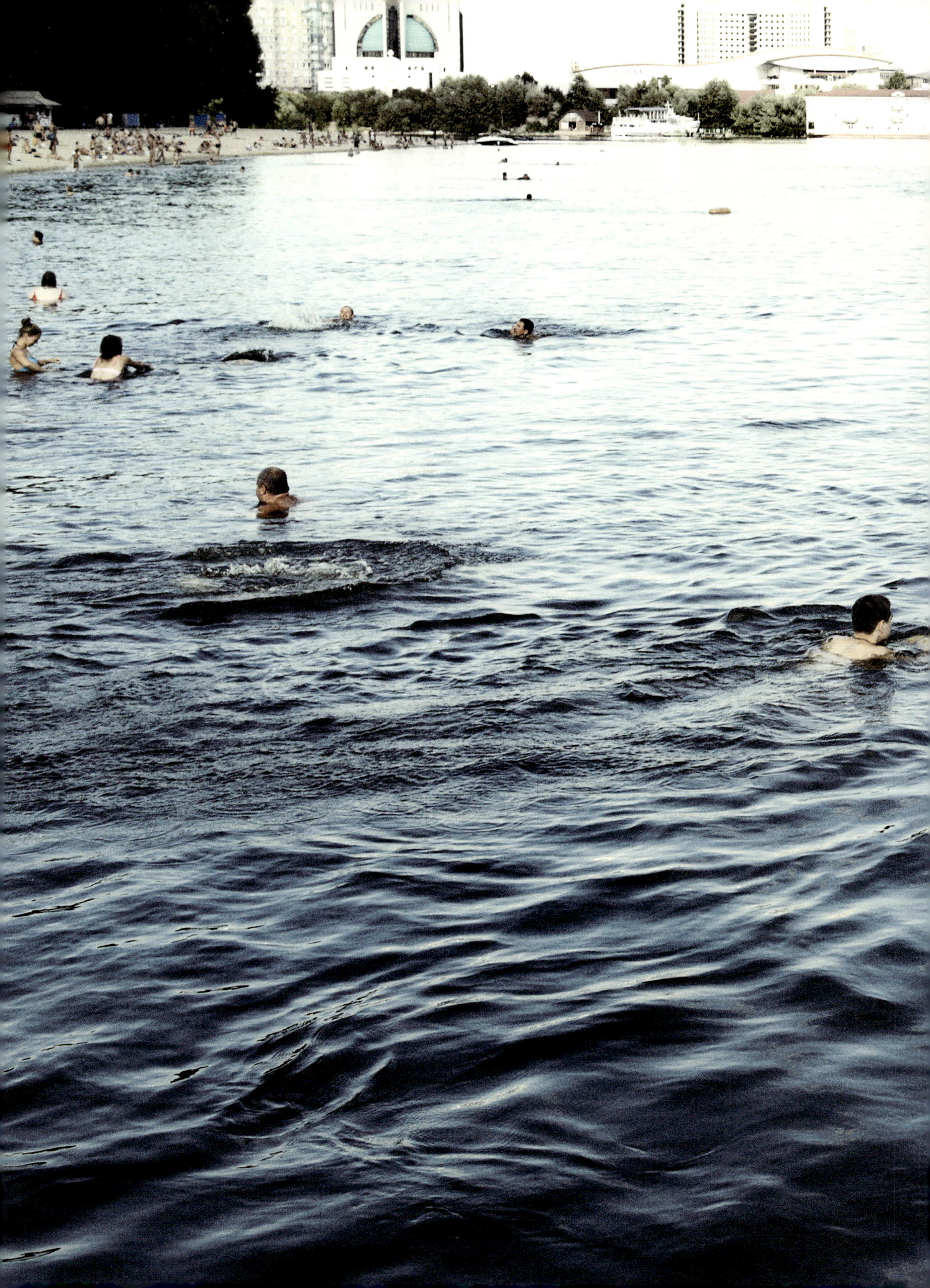

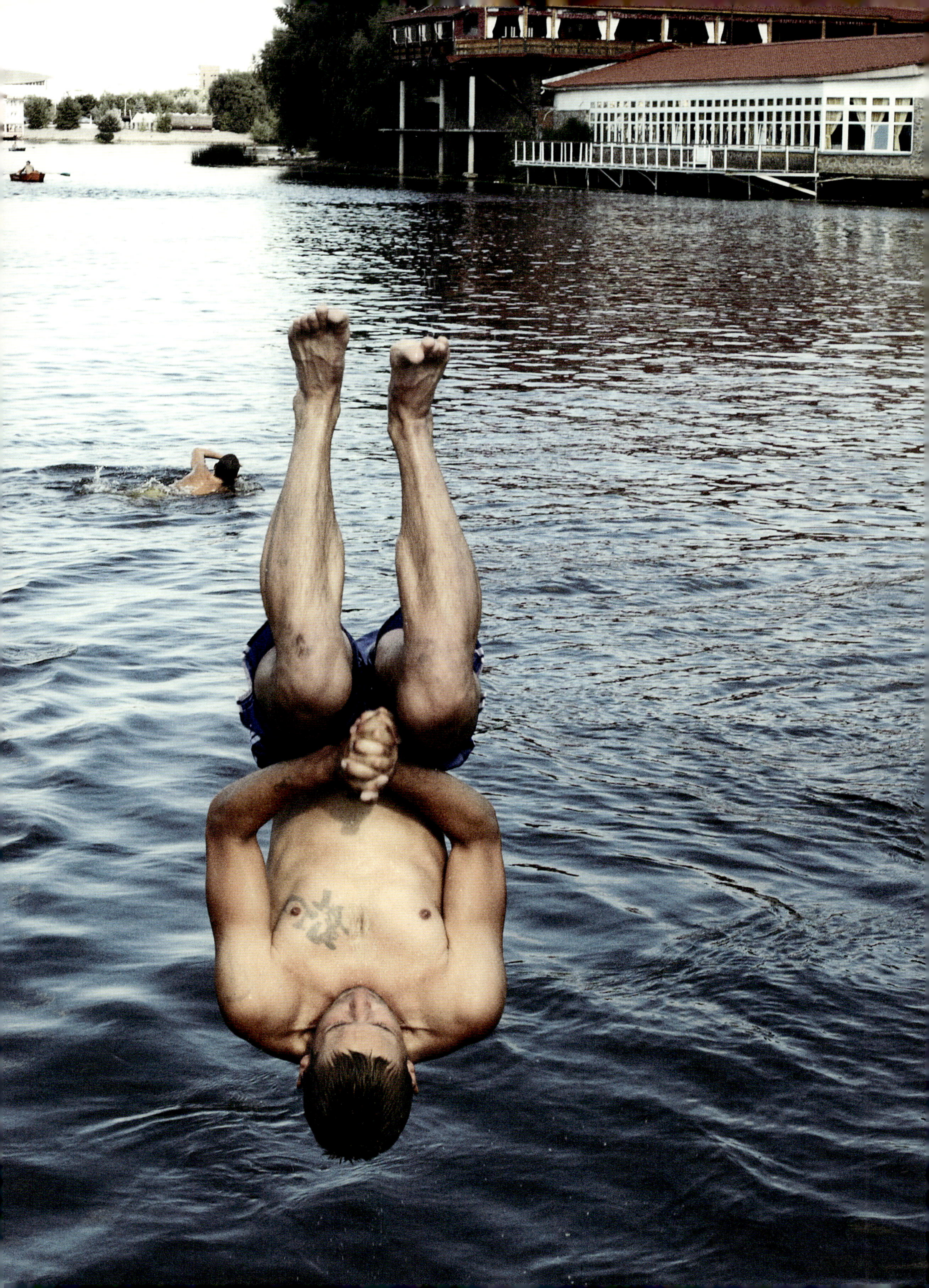

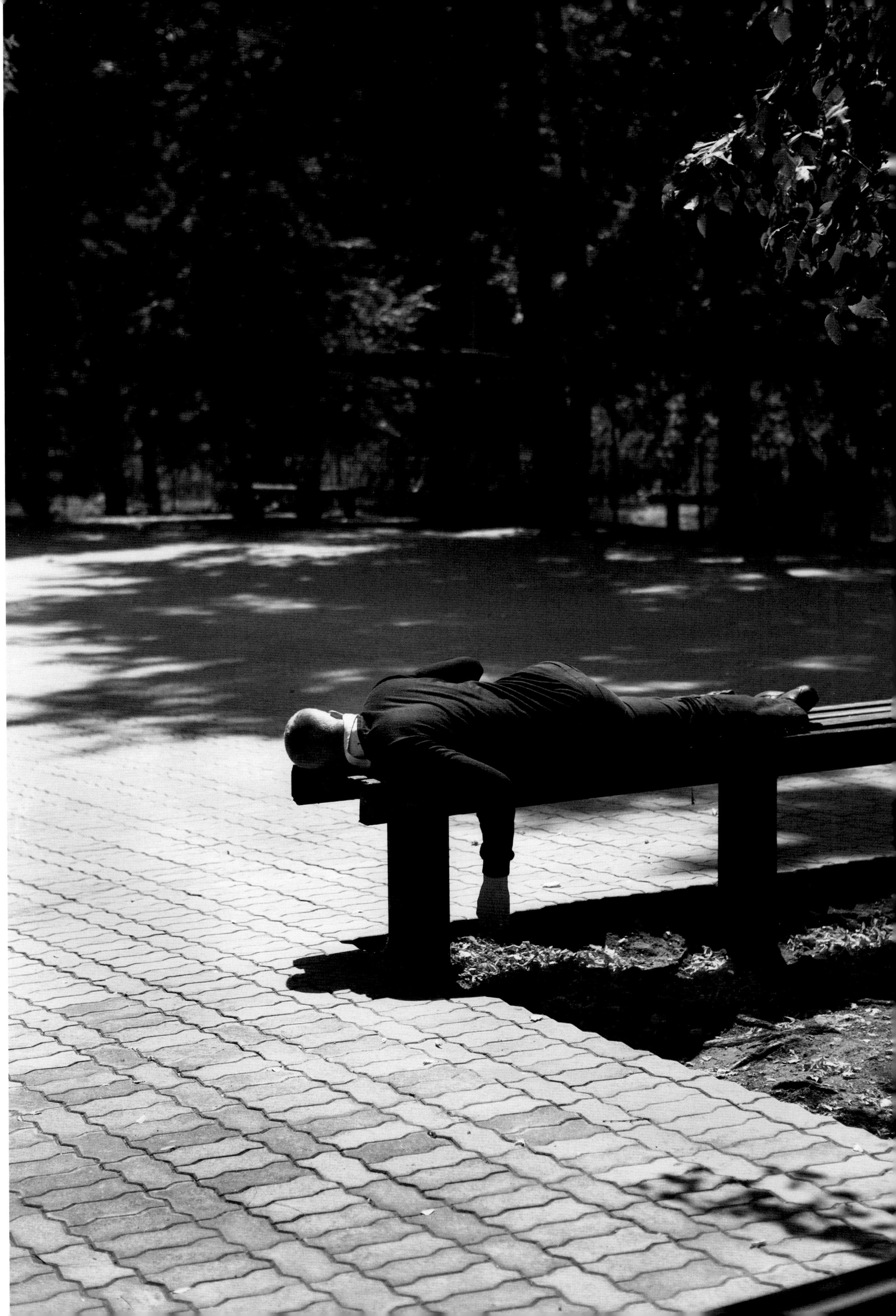

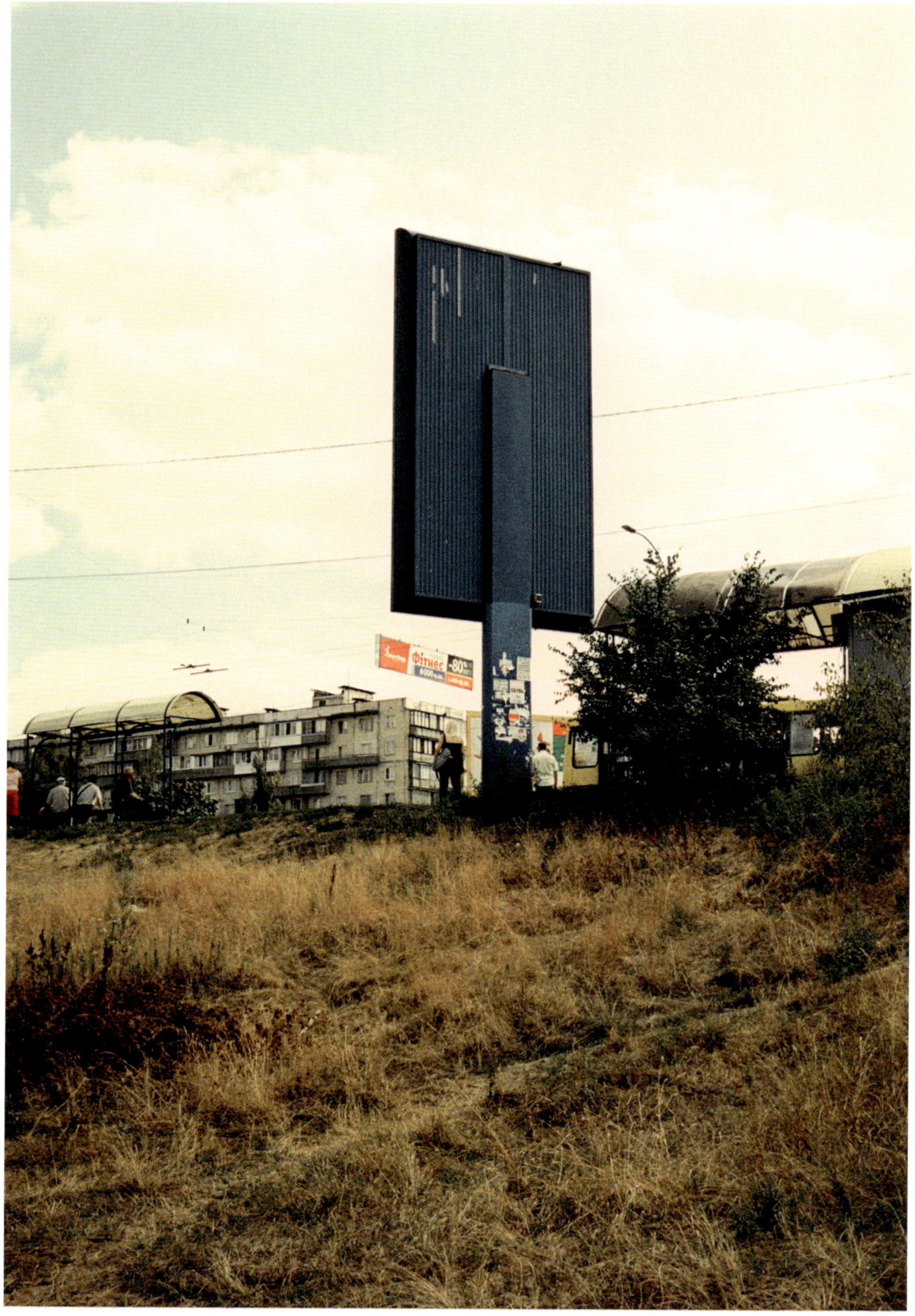
Фітнес
-80

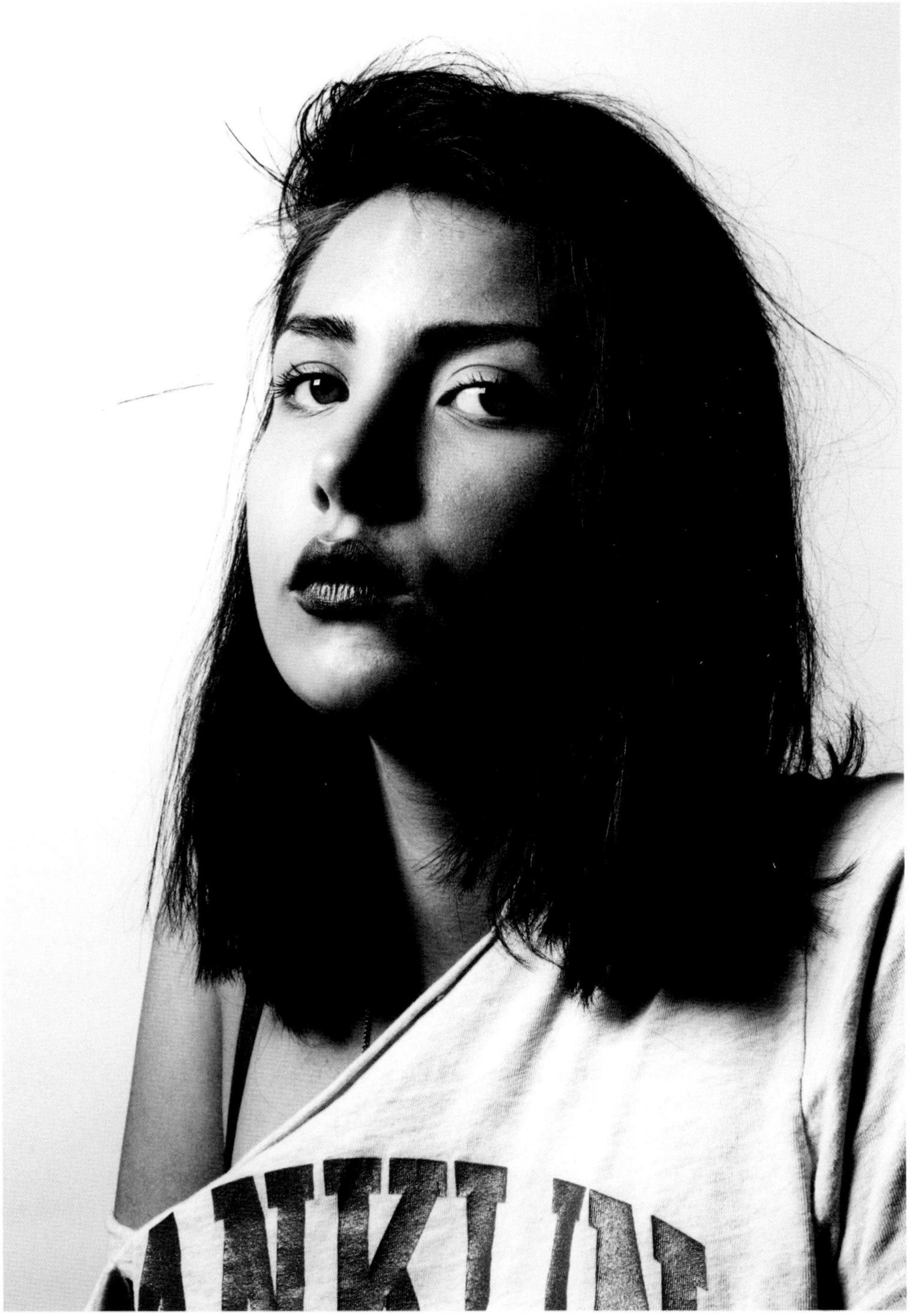

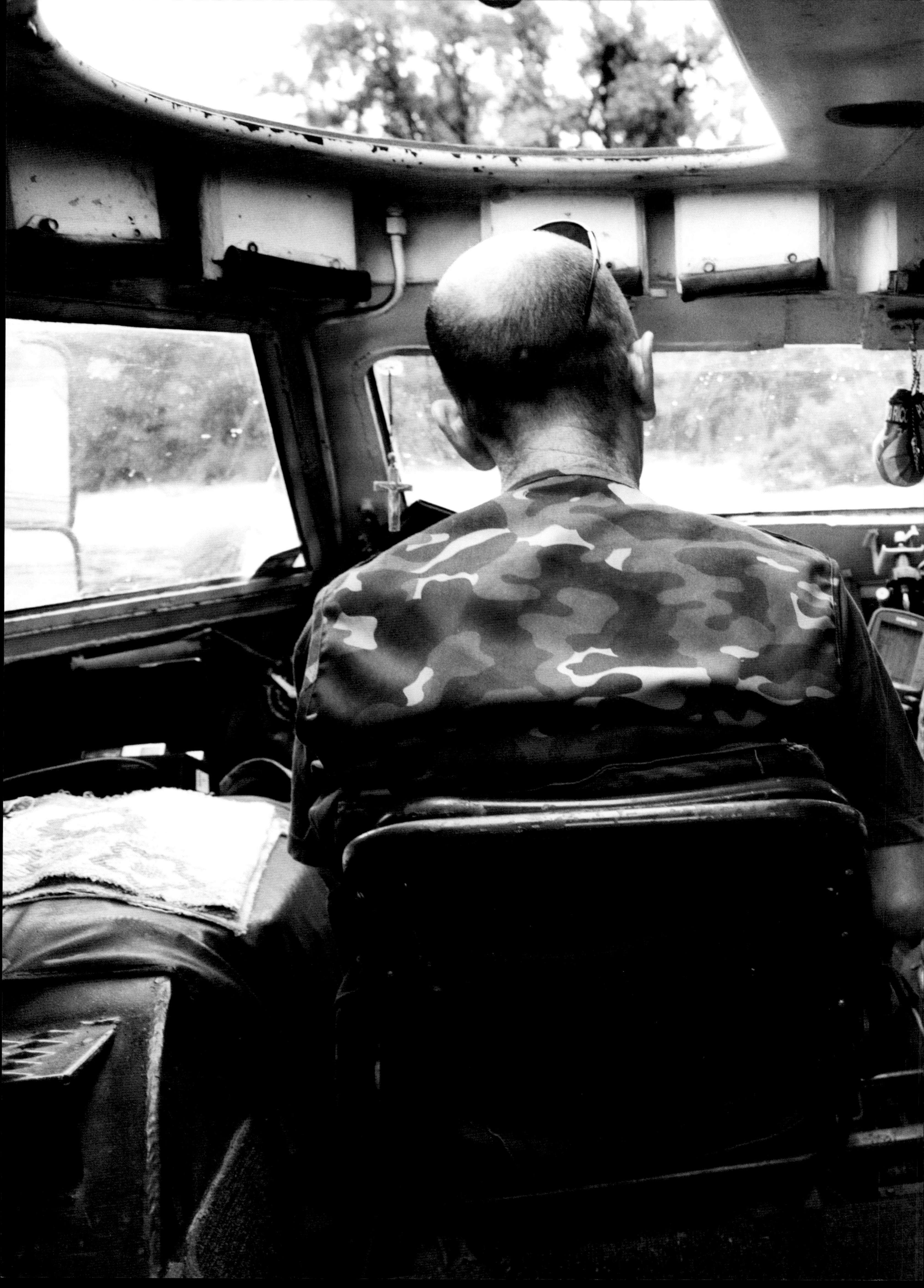

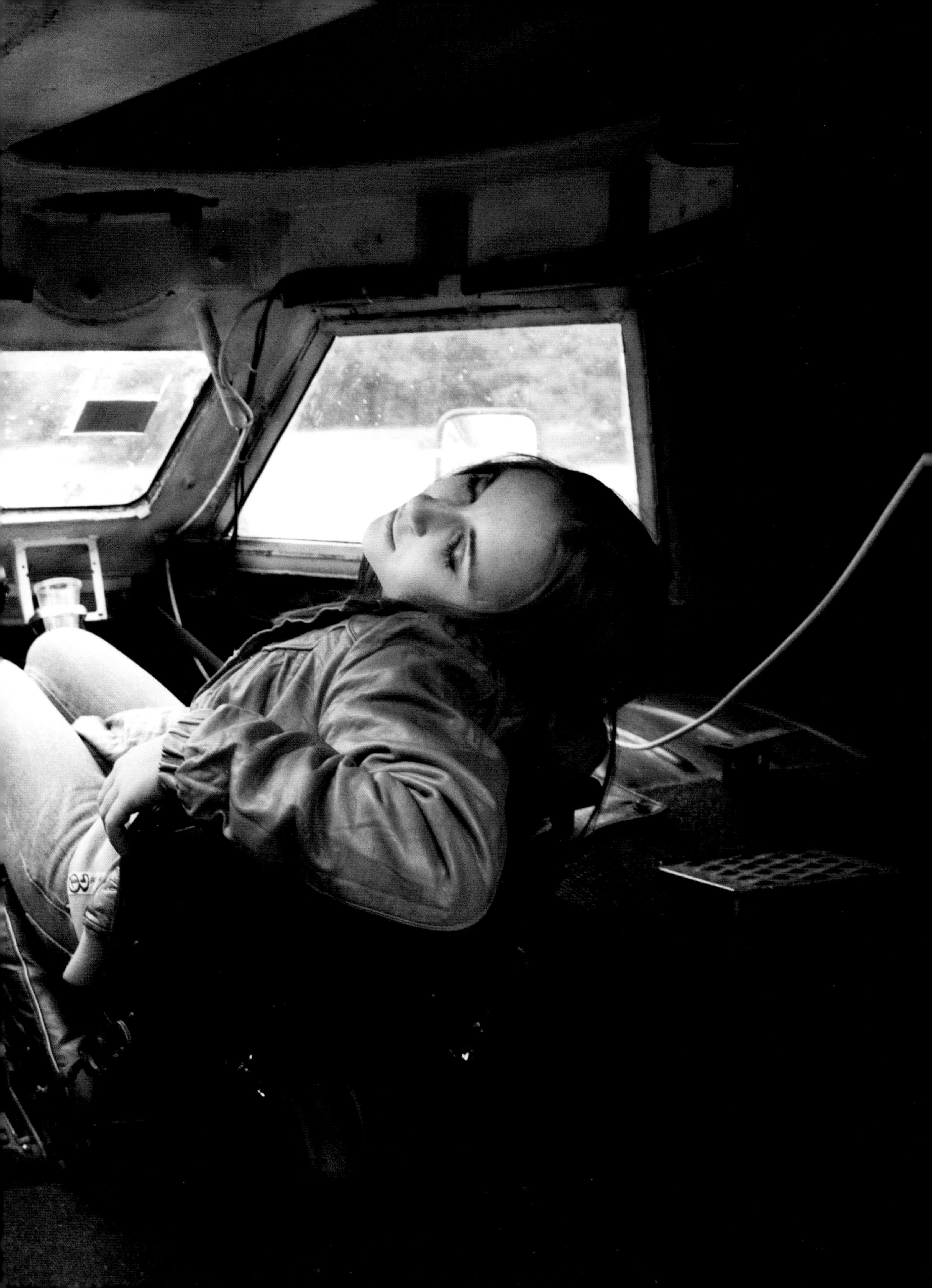

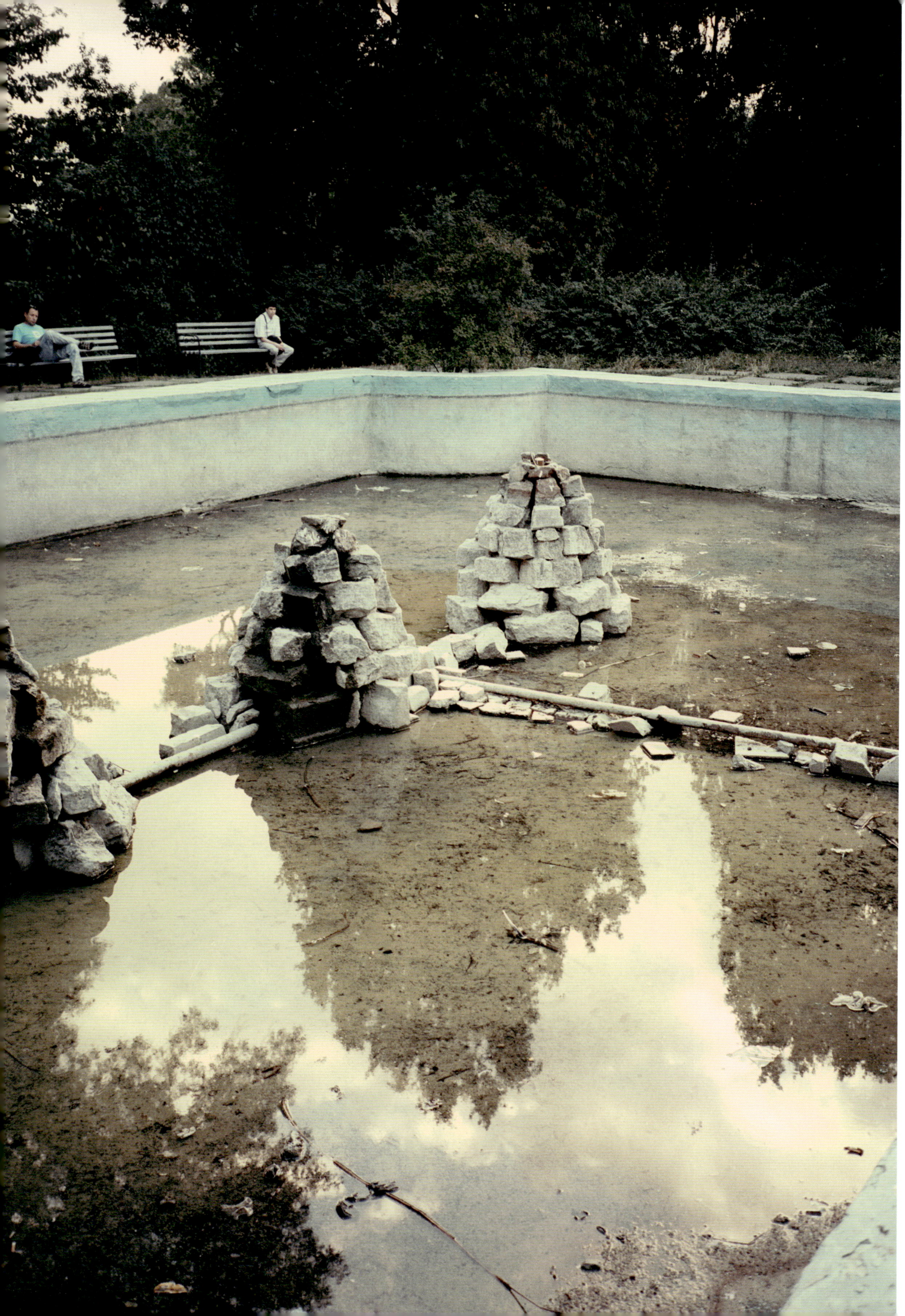

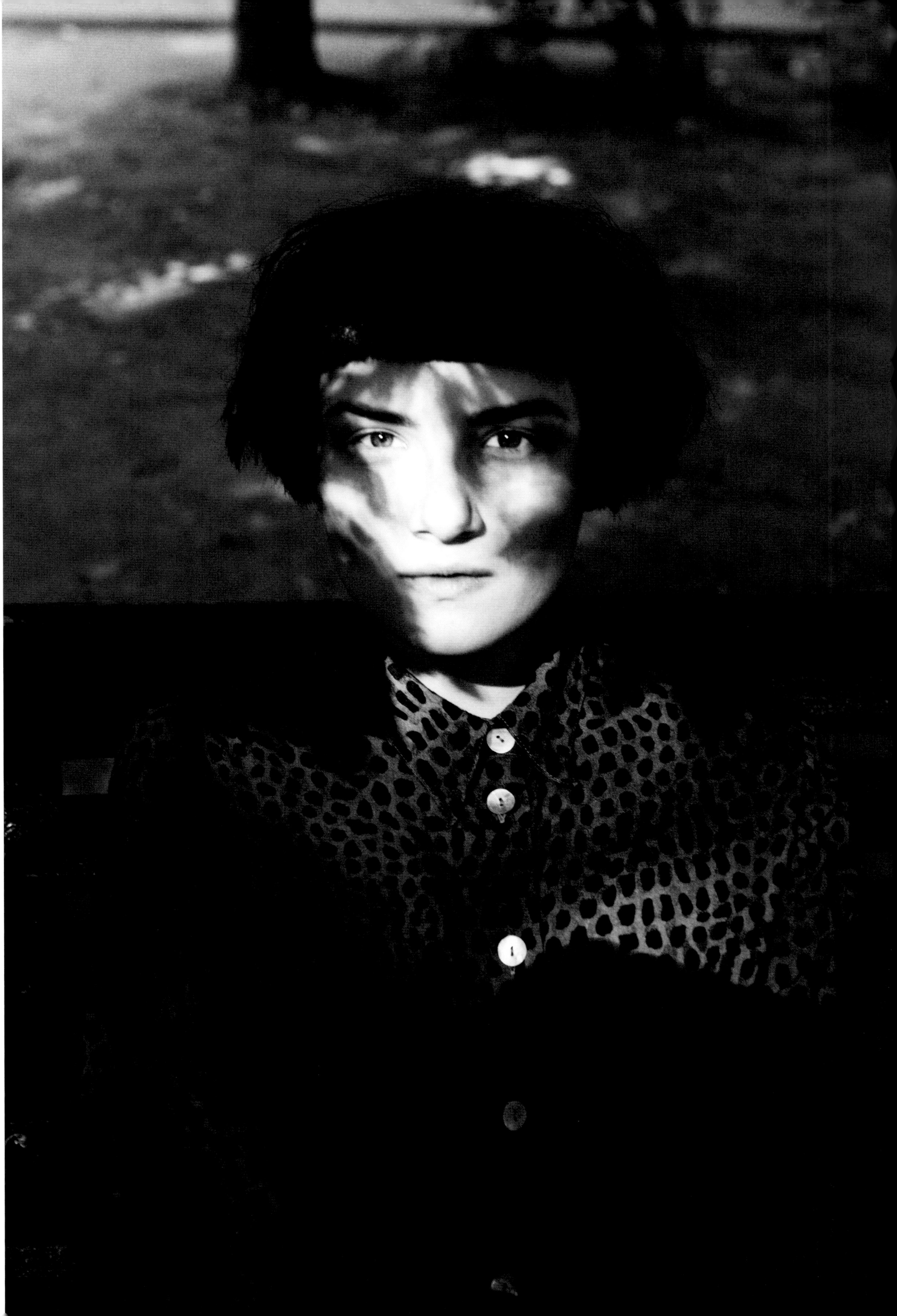

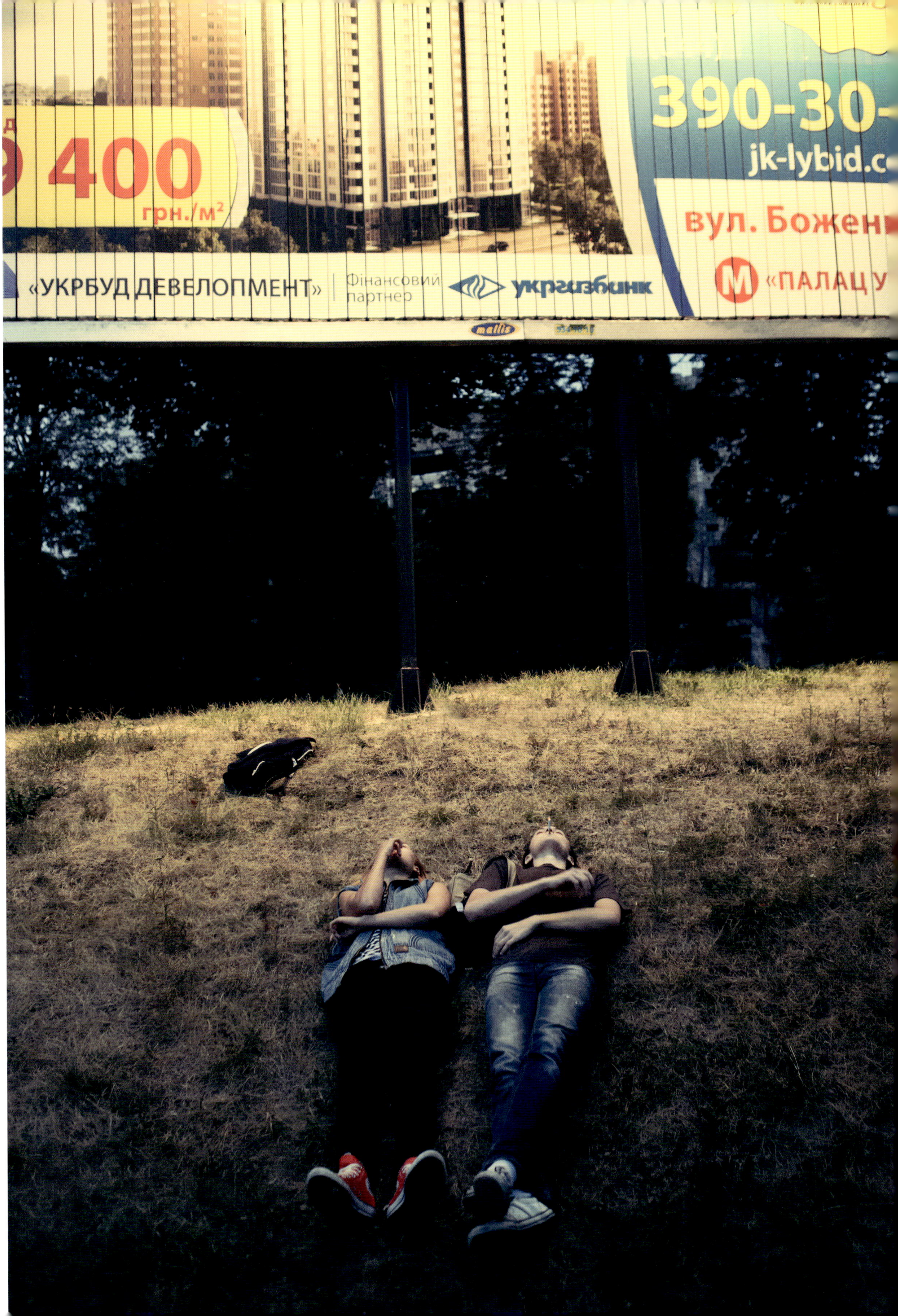
400
грн./м²
«УКРБУД ДЕВЕЛОПМЕНТ»
Фінансовий партнер
укргазбанк

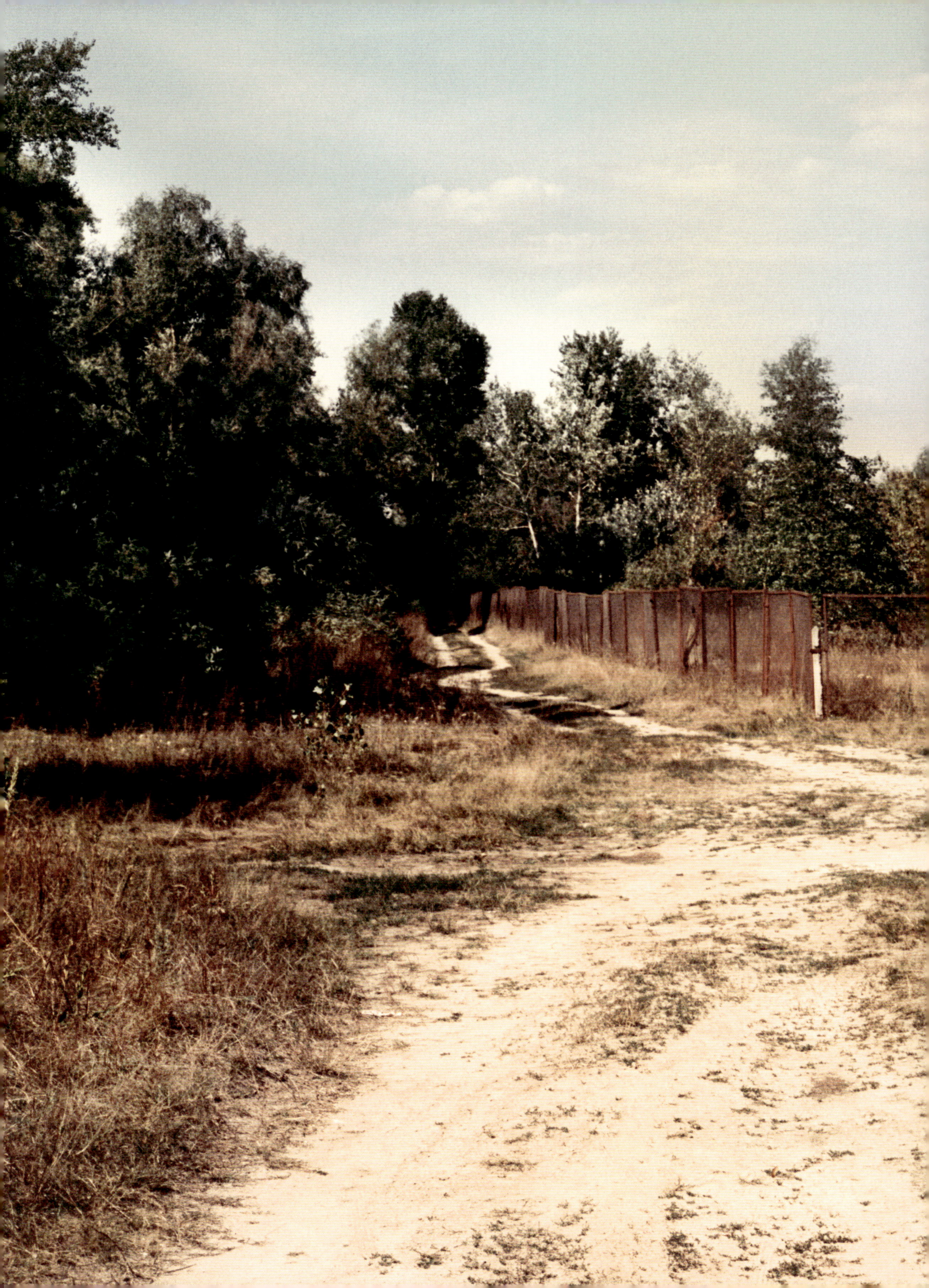

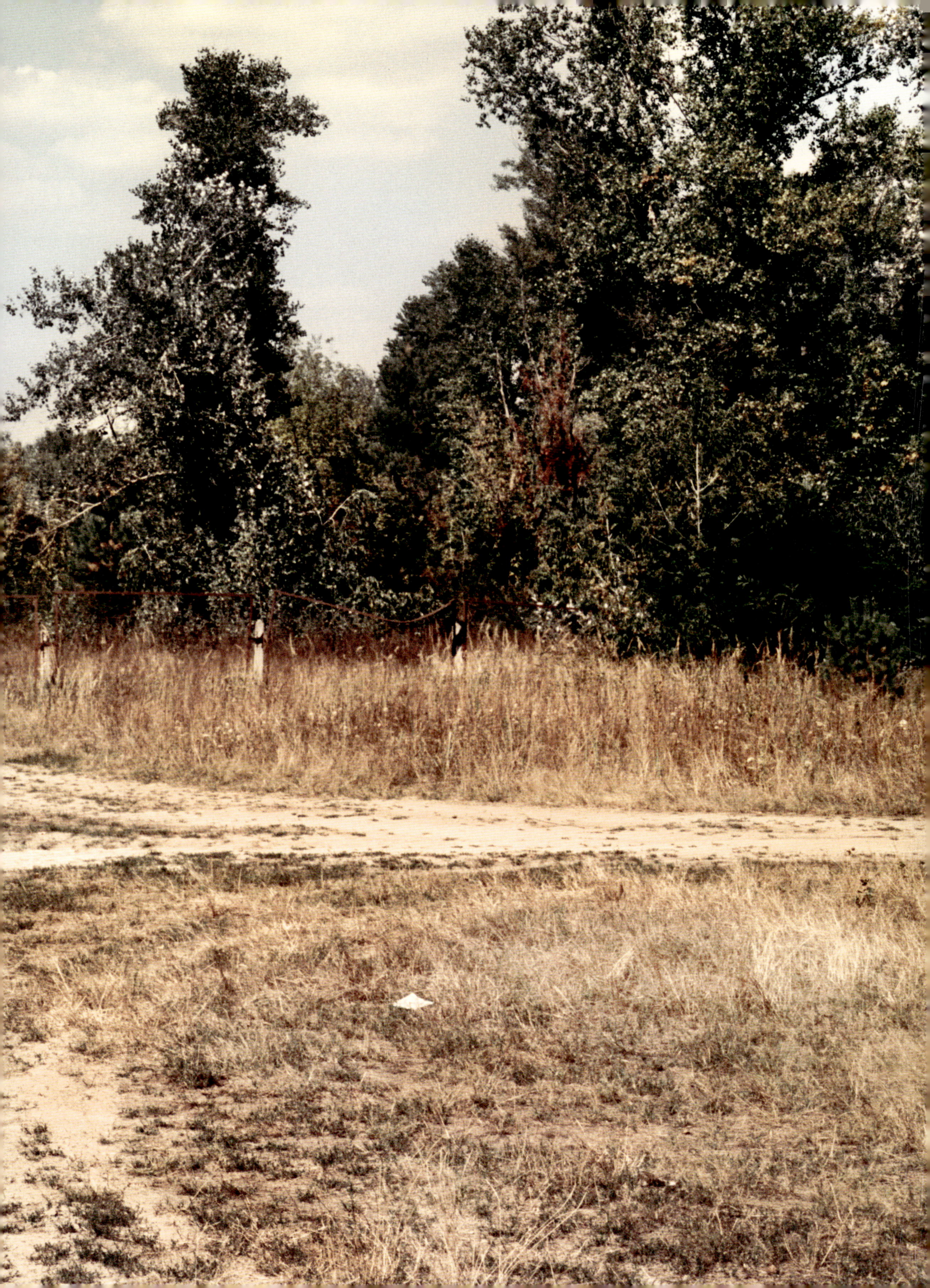

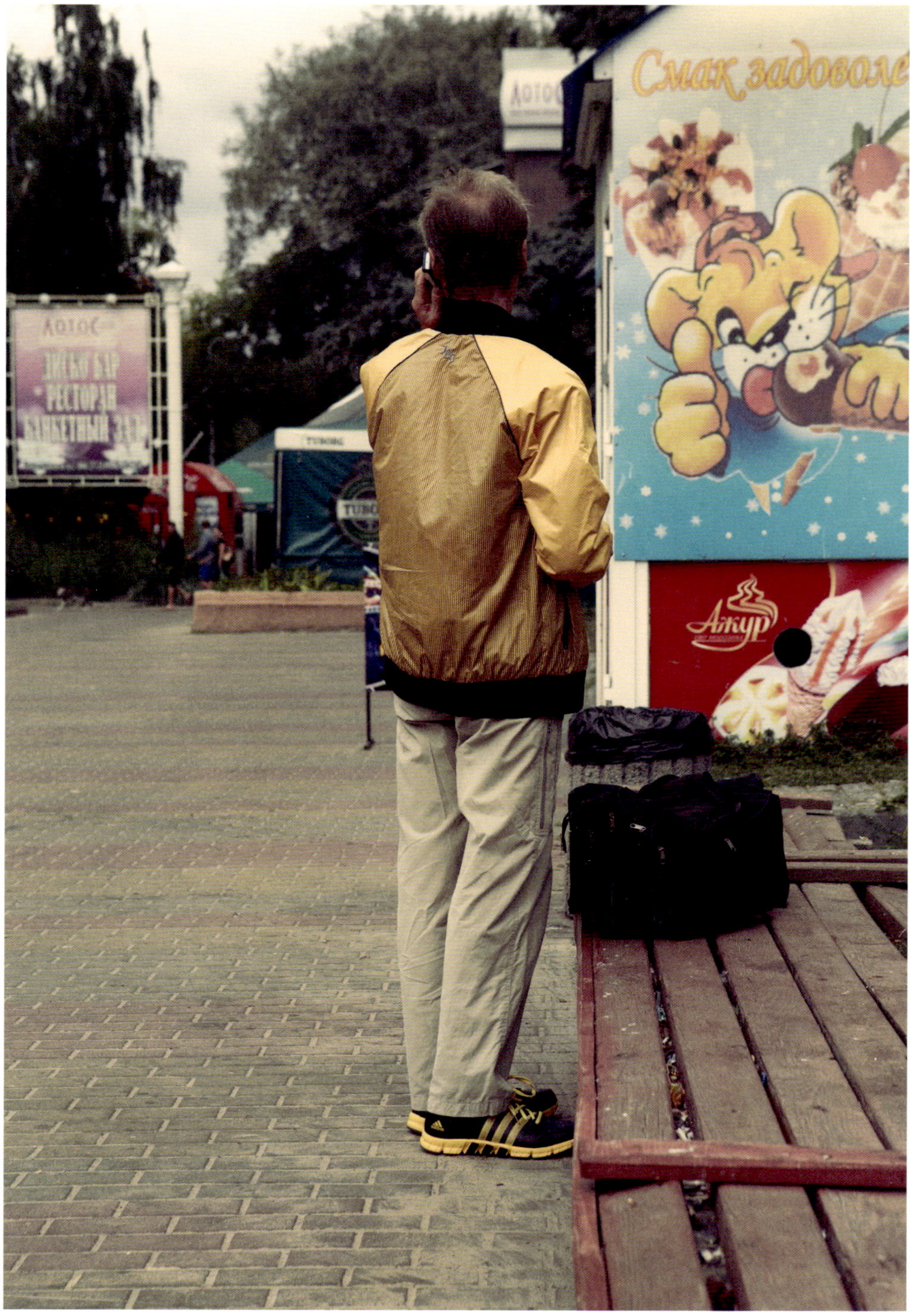
Ажур
TUBORG

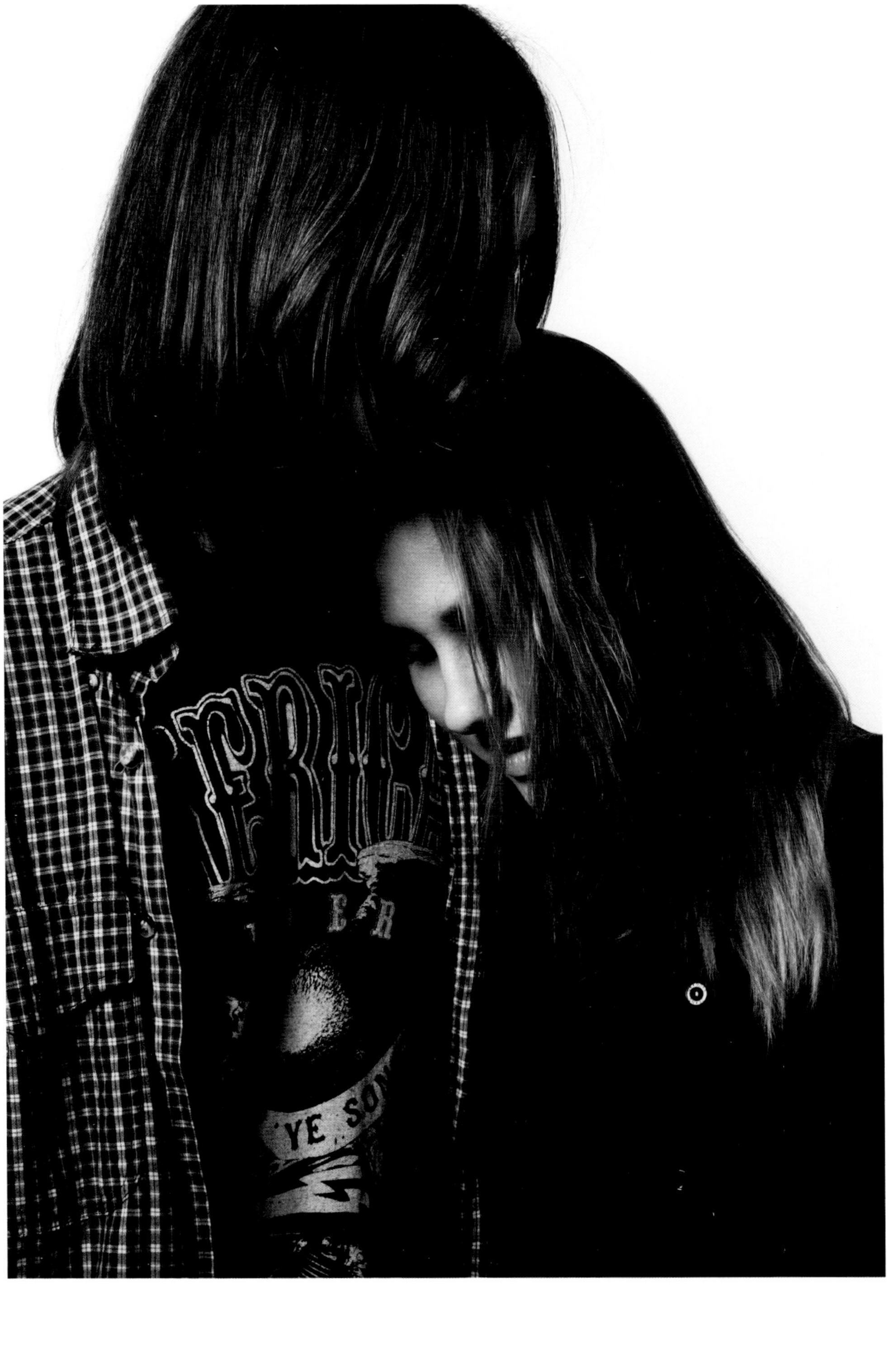

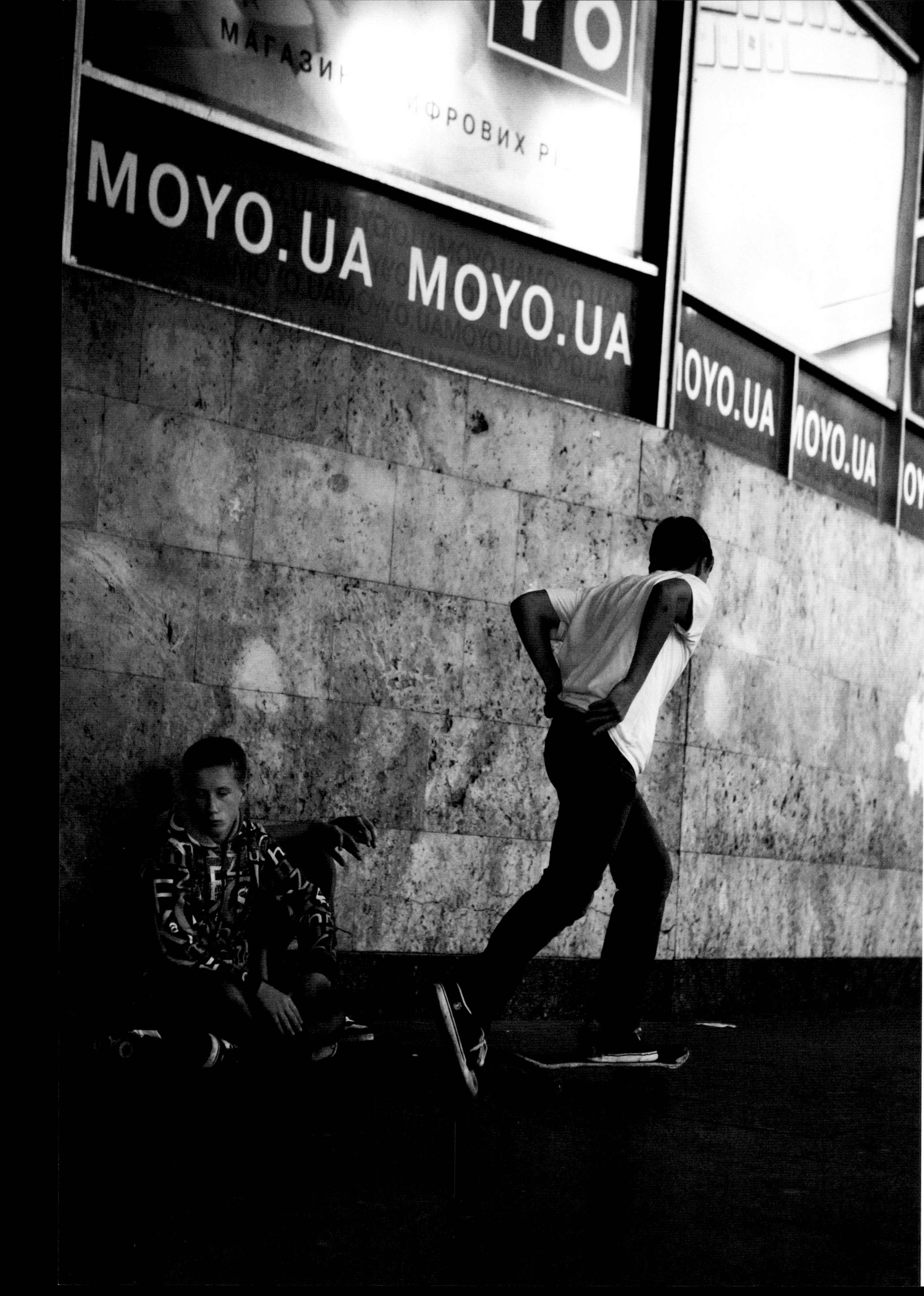
MOYO.UA MOYO.UA

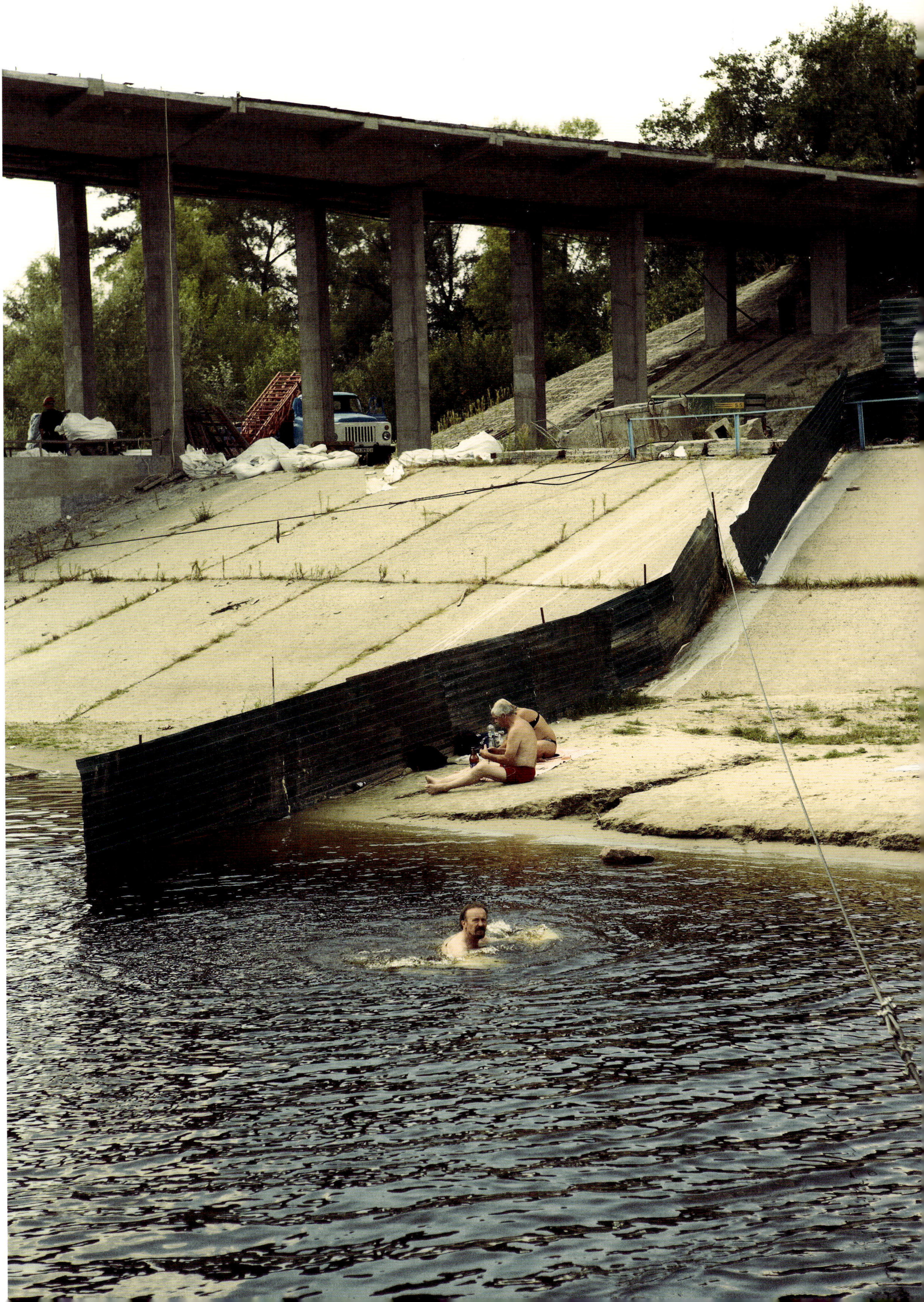

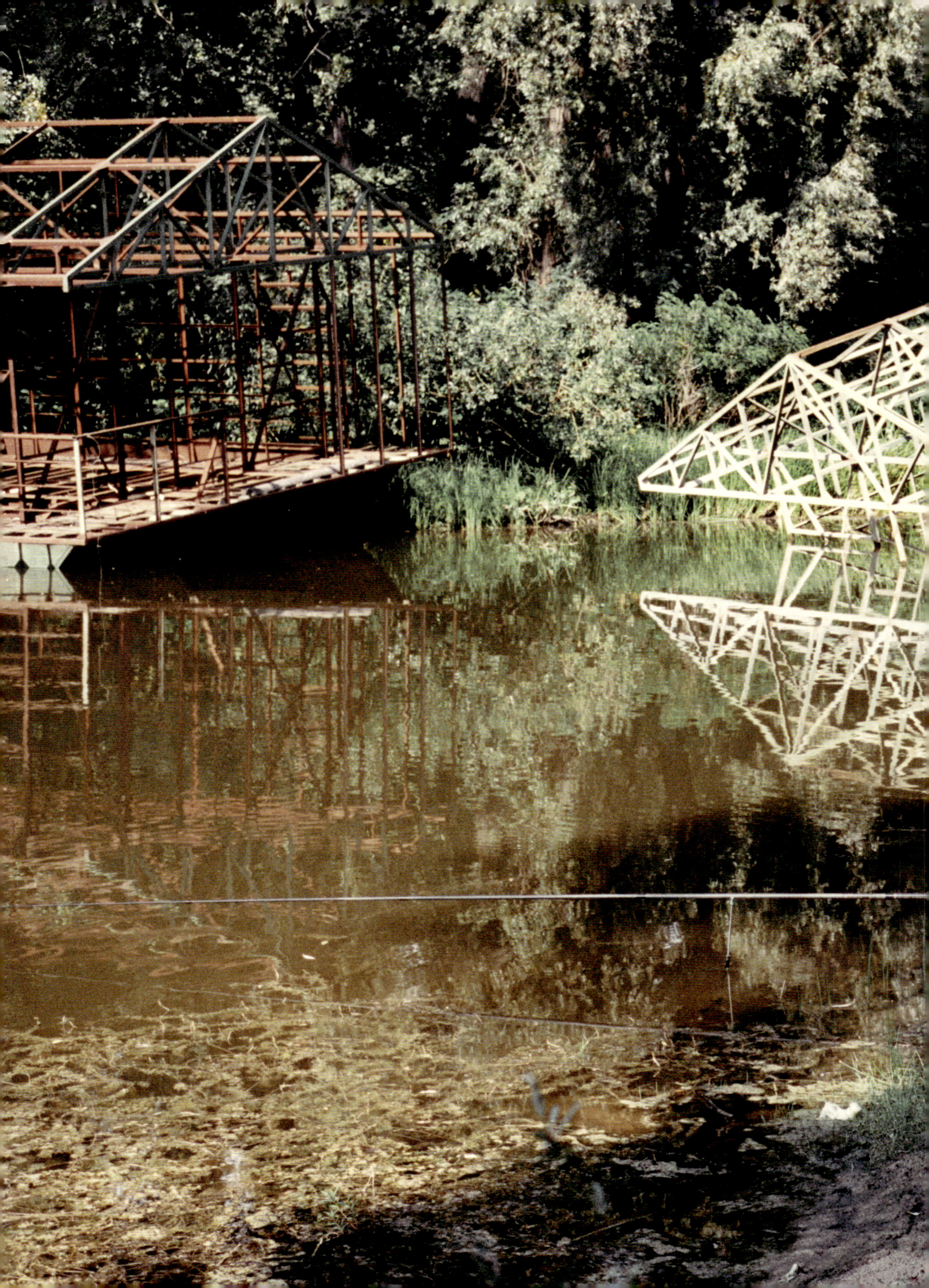

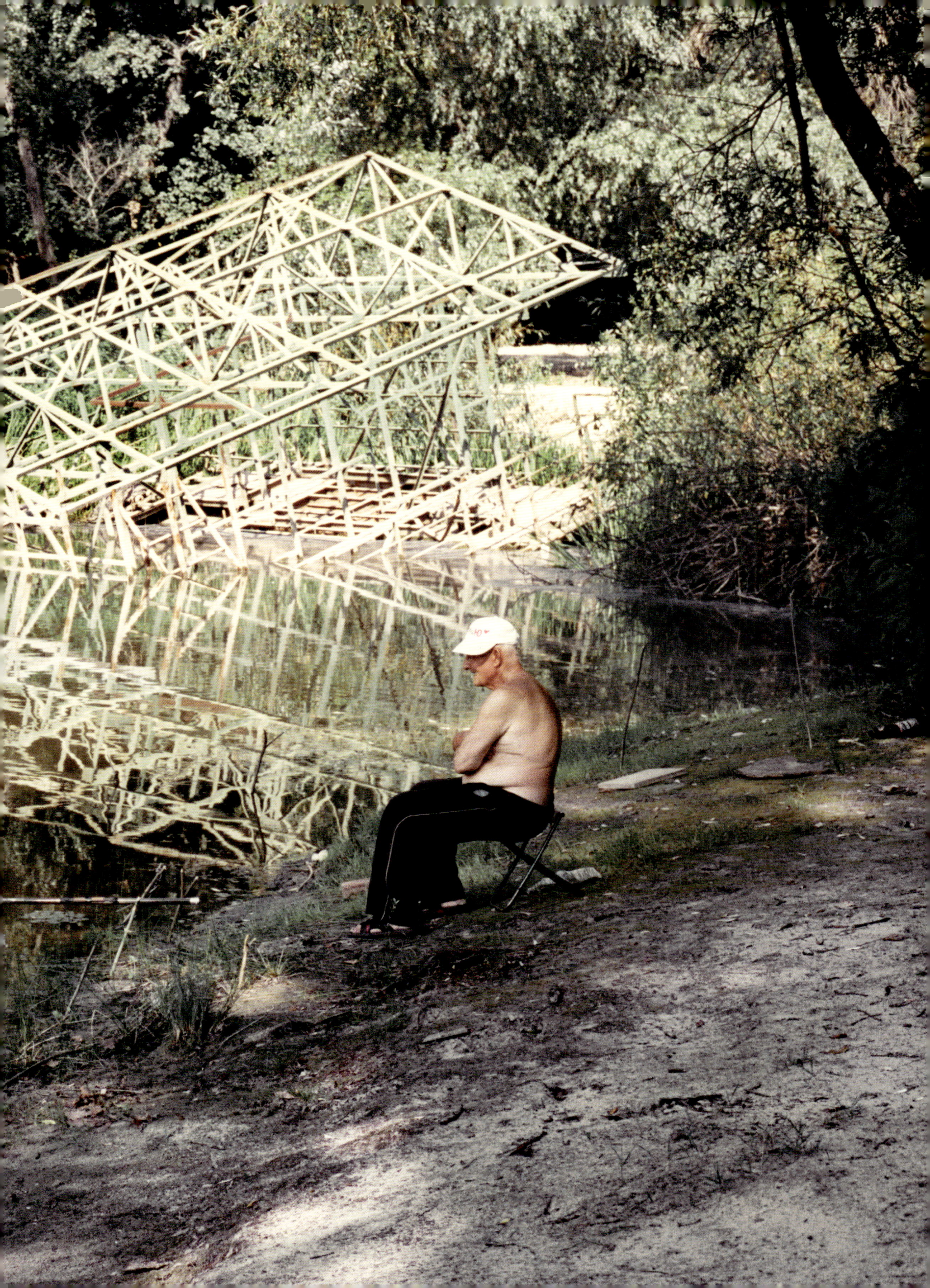

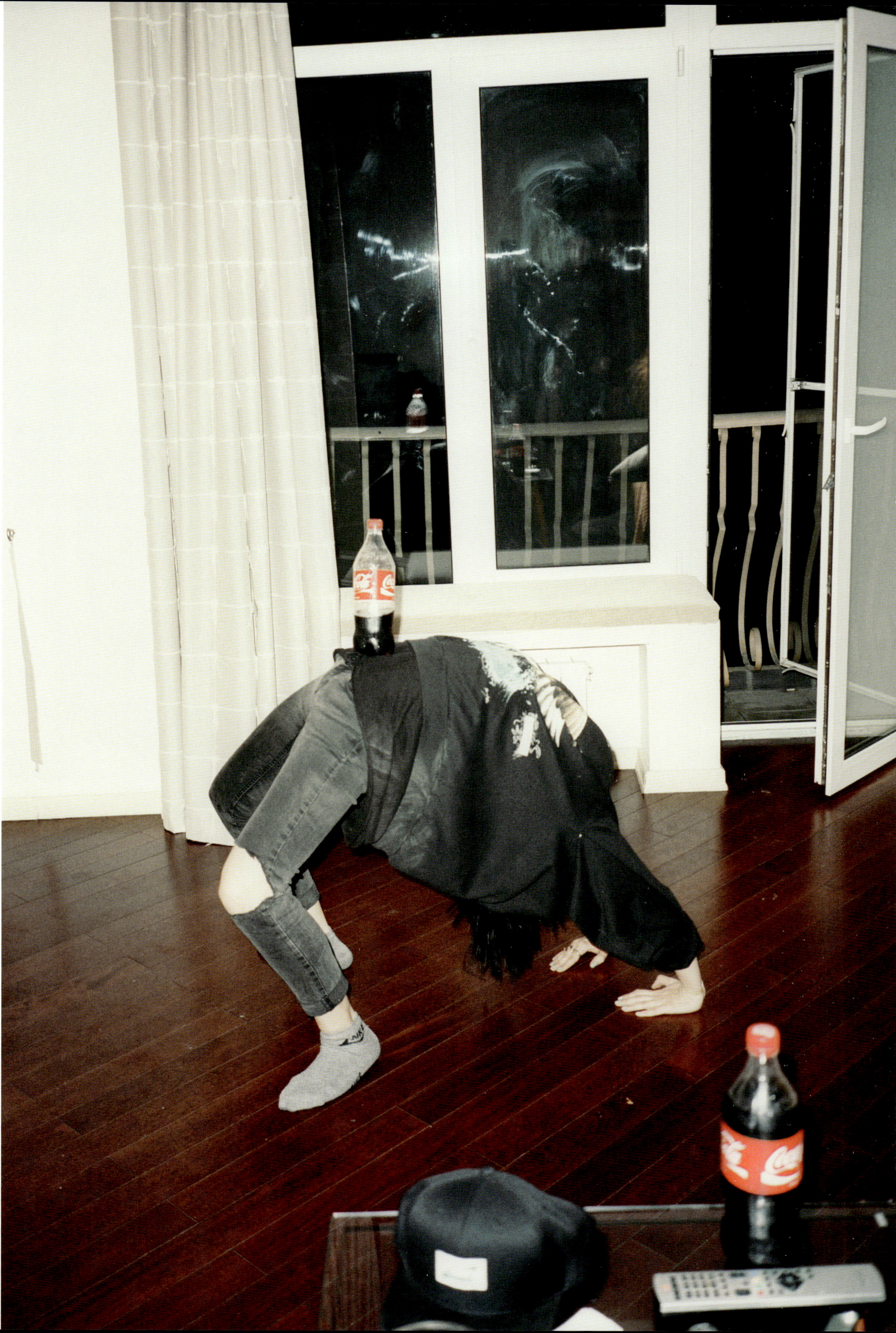

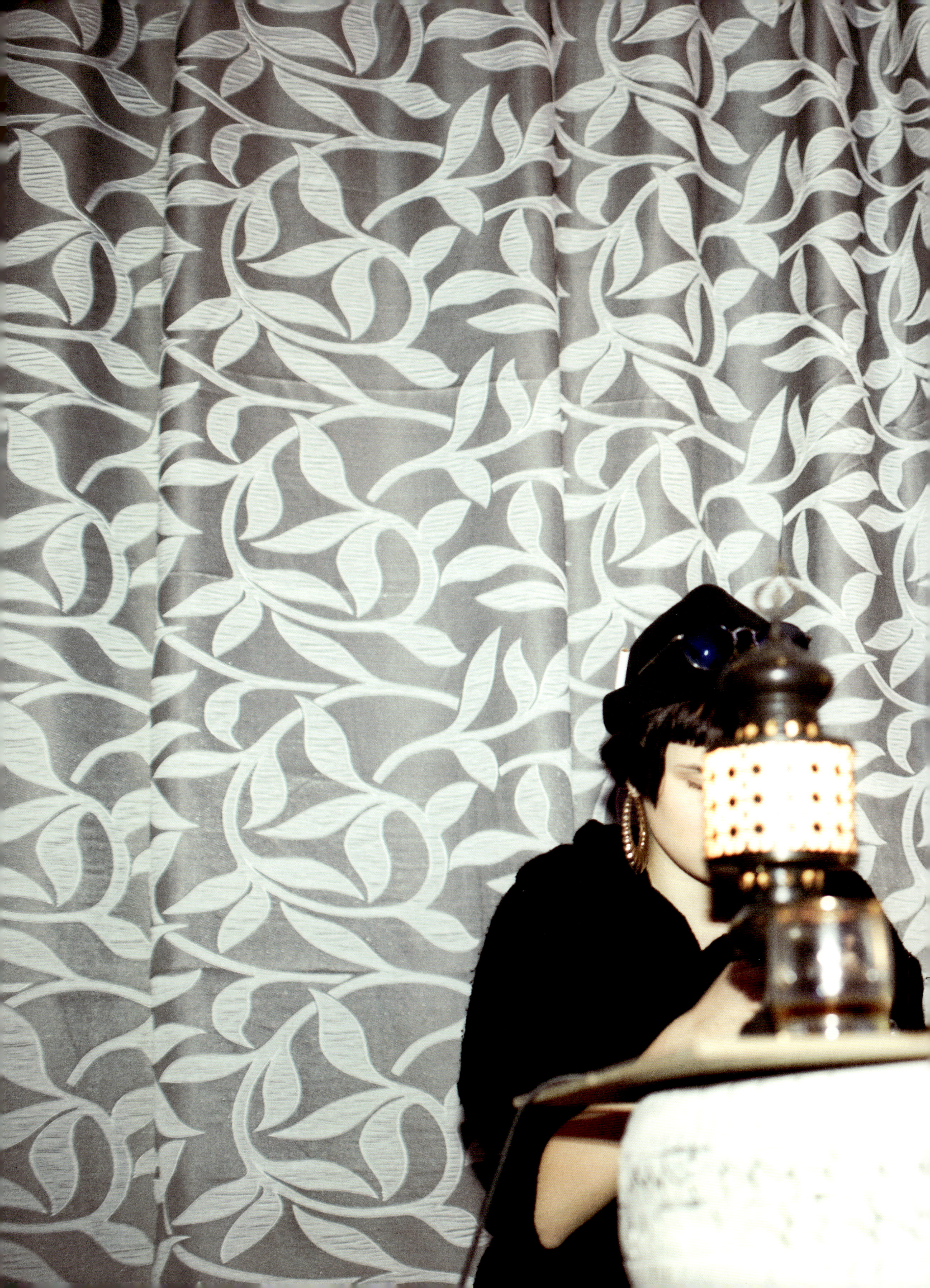

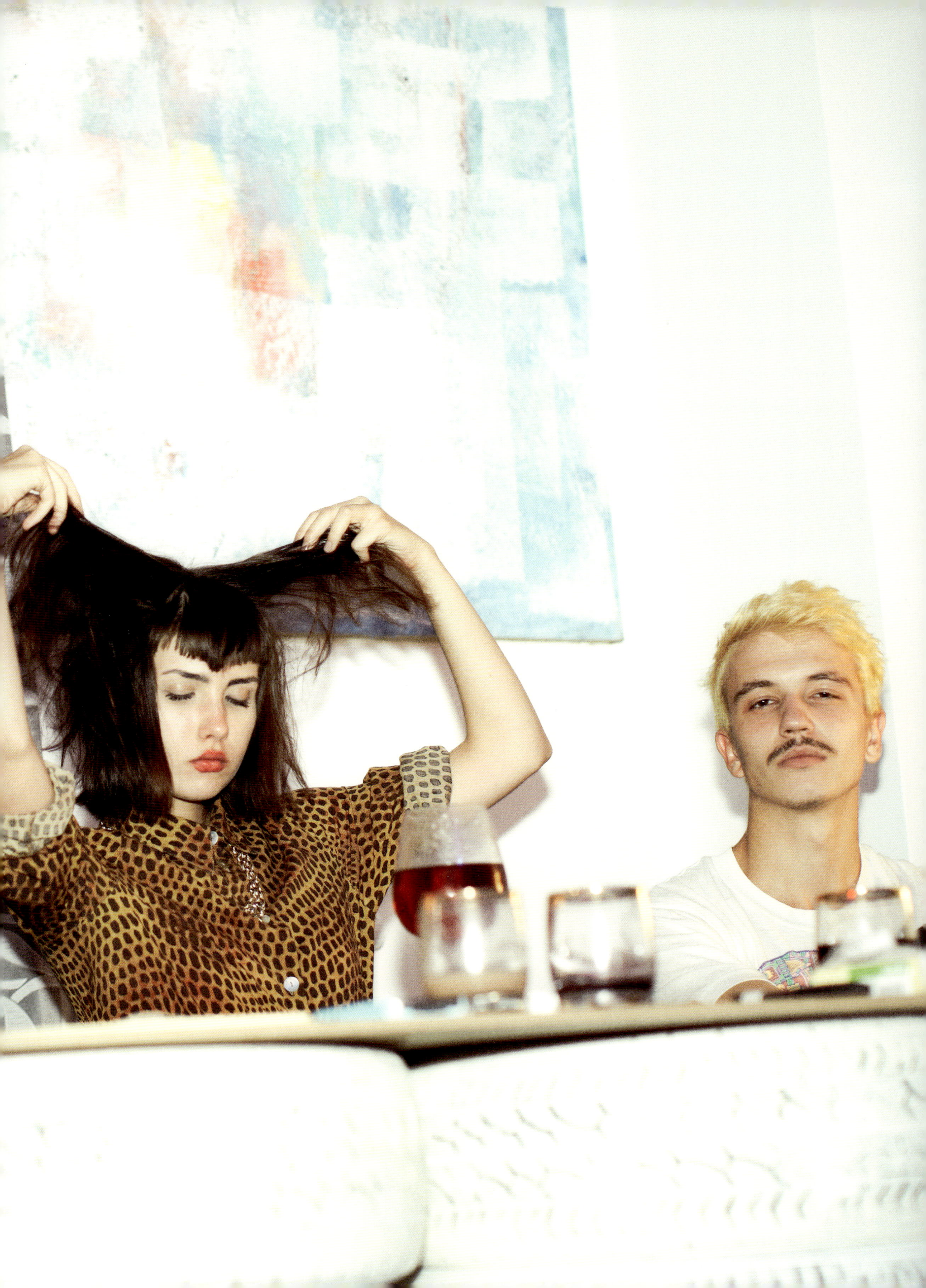

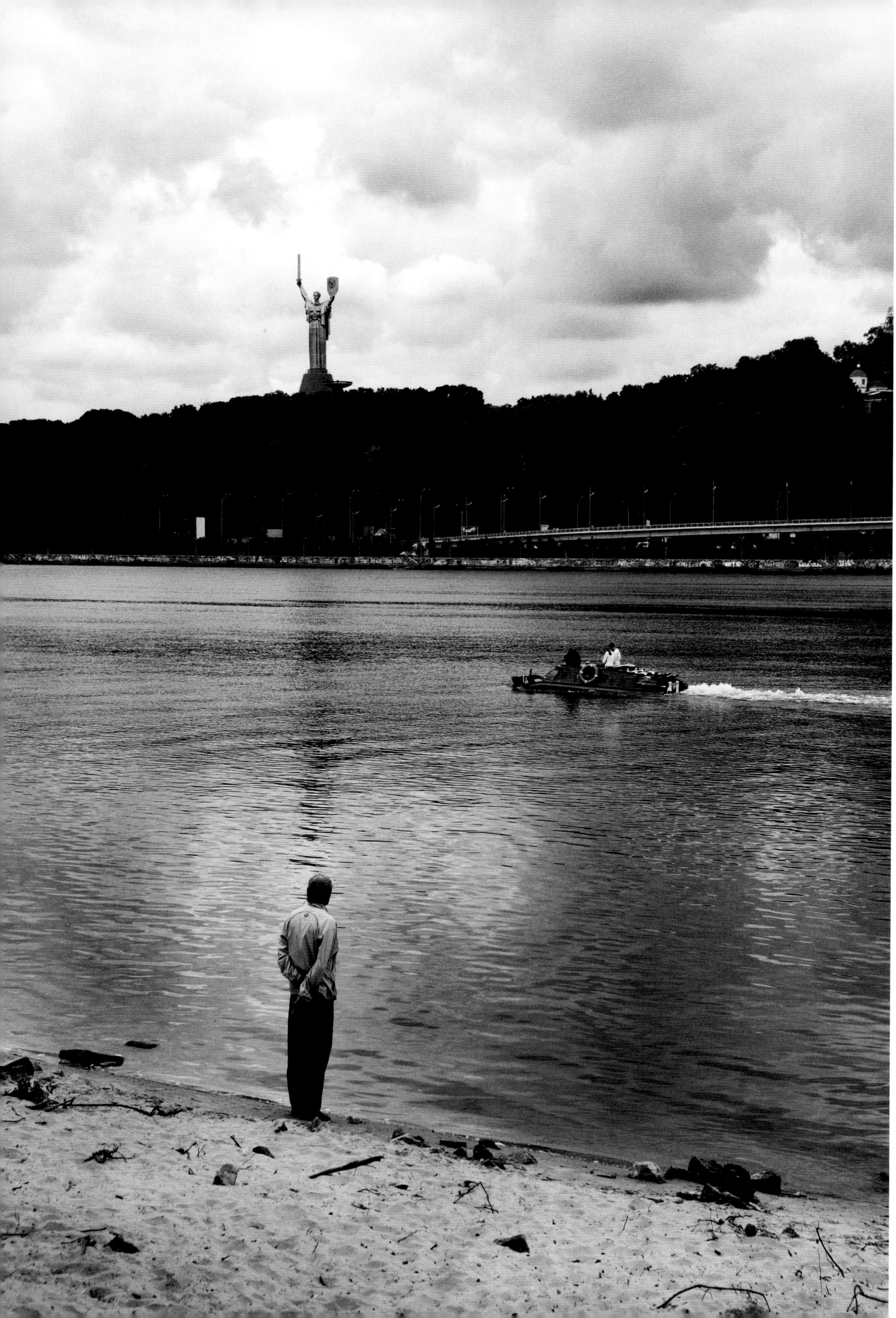

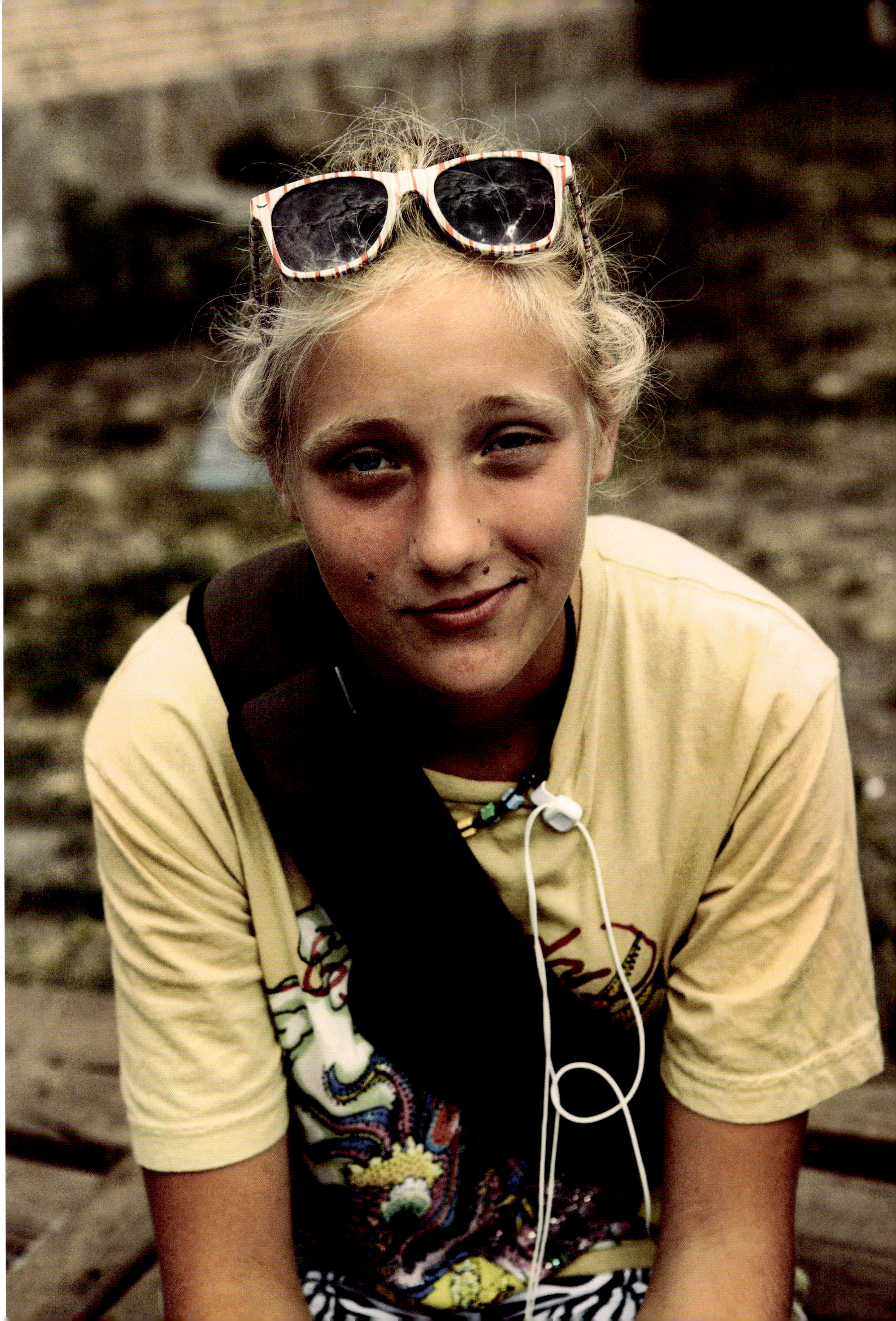

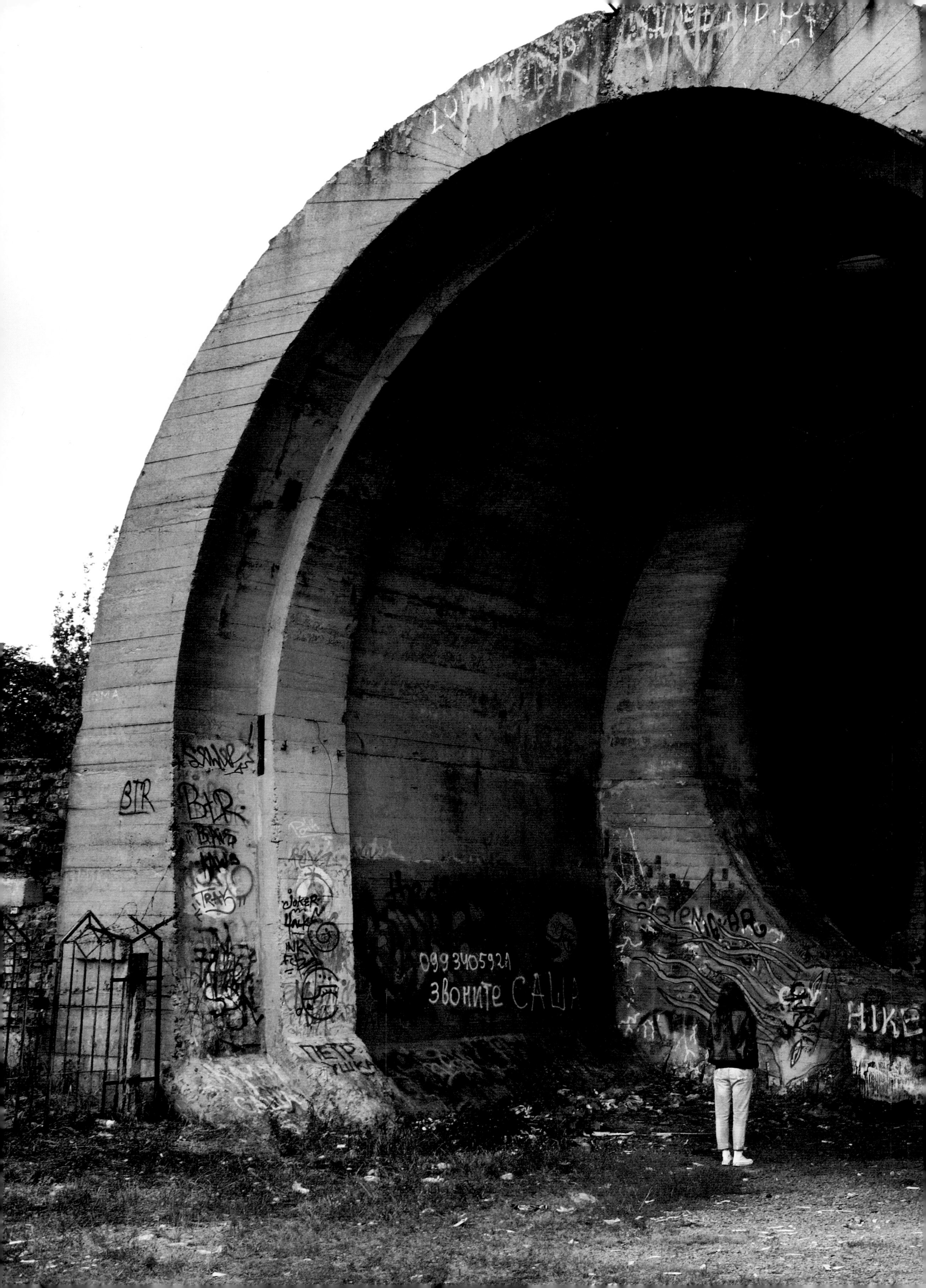
BTR
0993405921
звоните САШ
HIKE

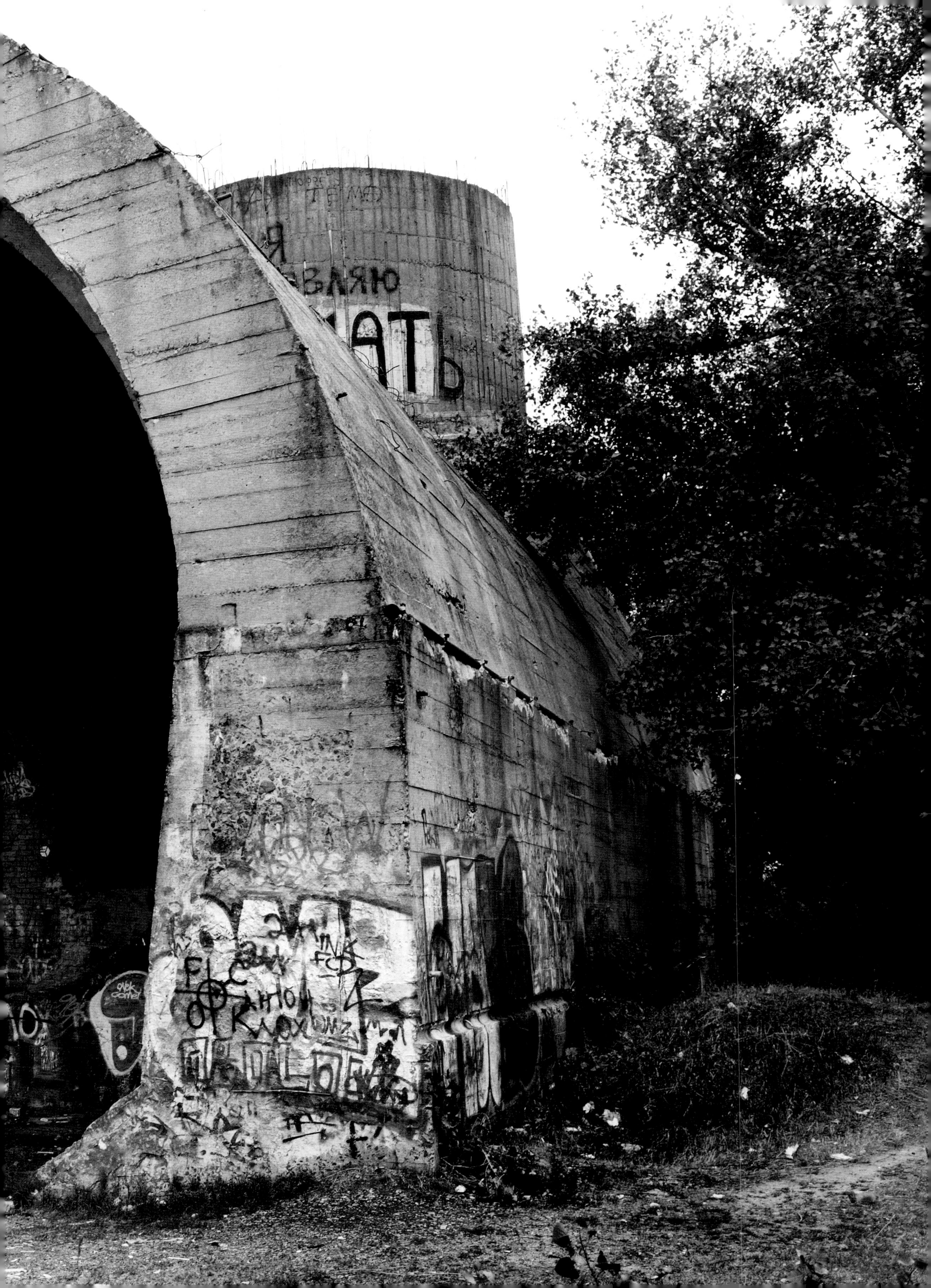

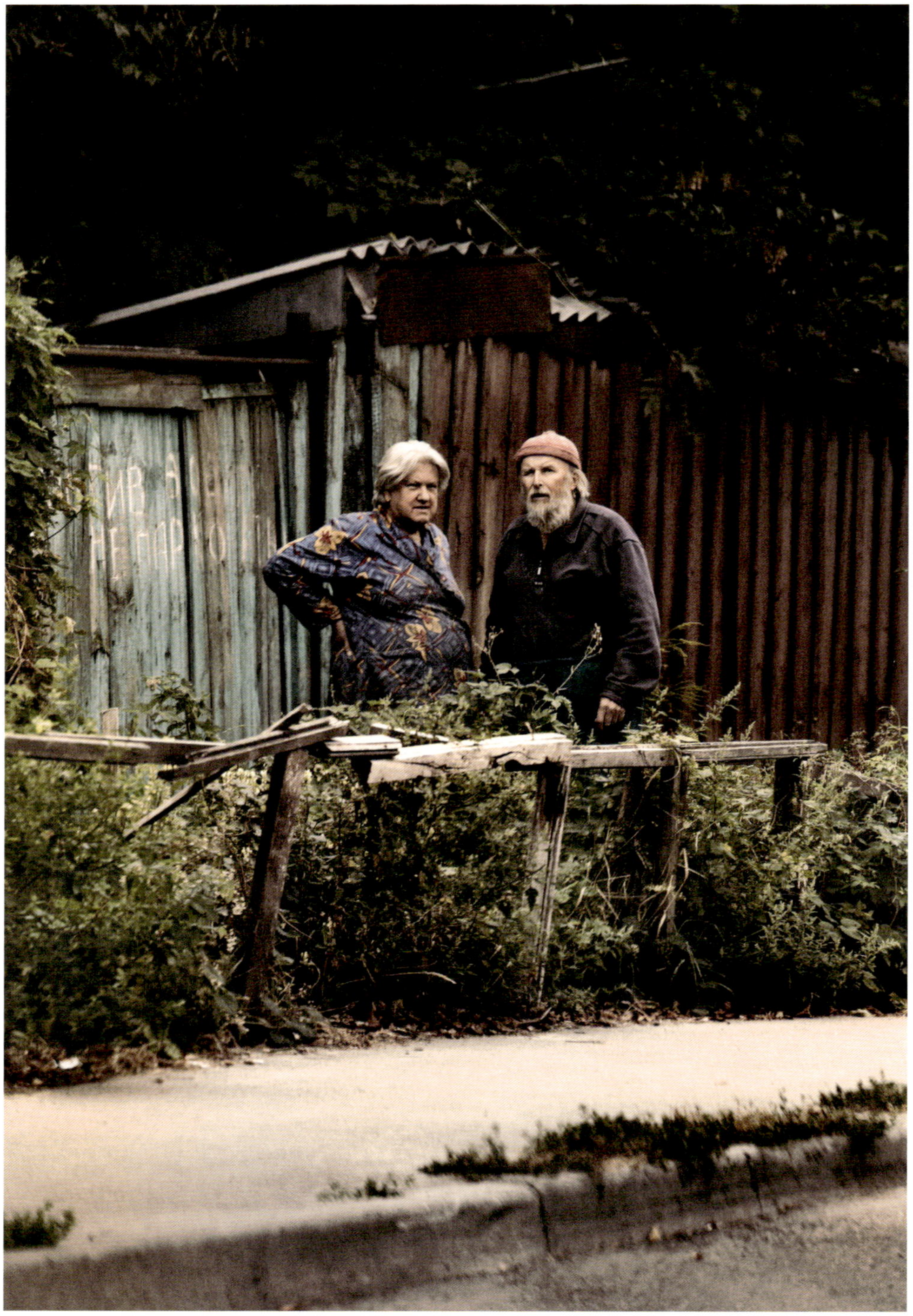

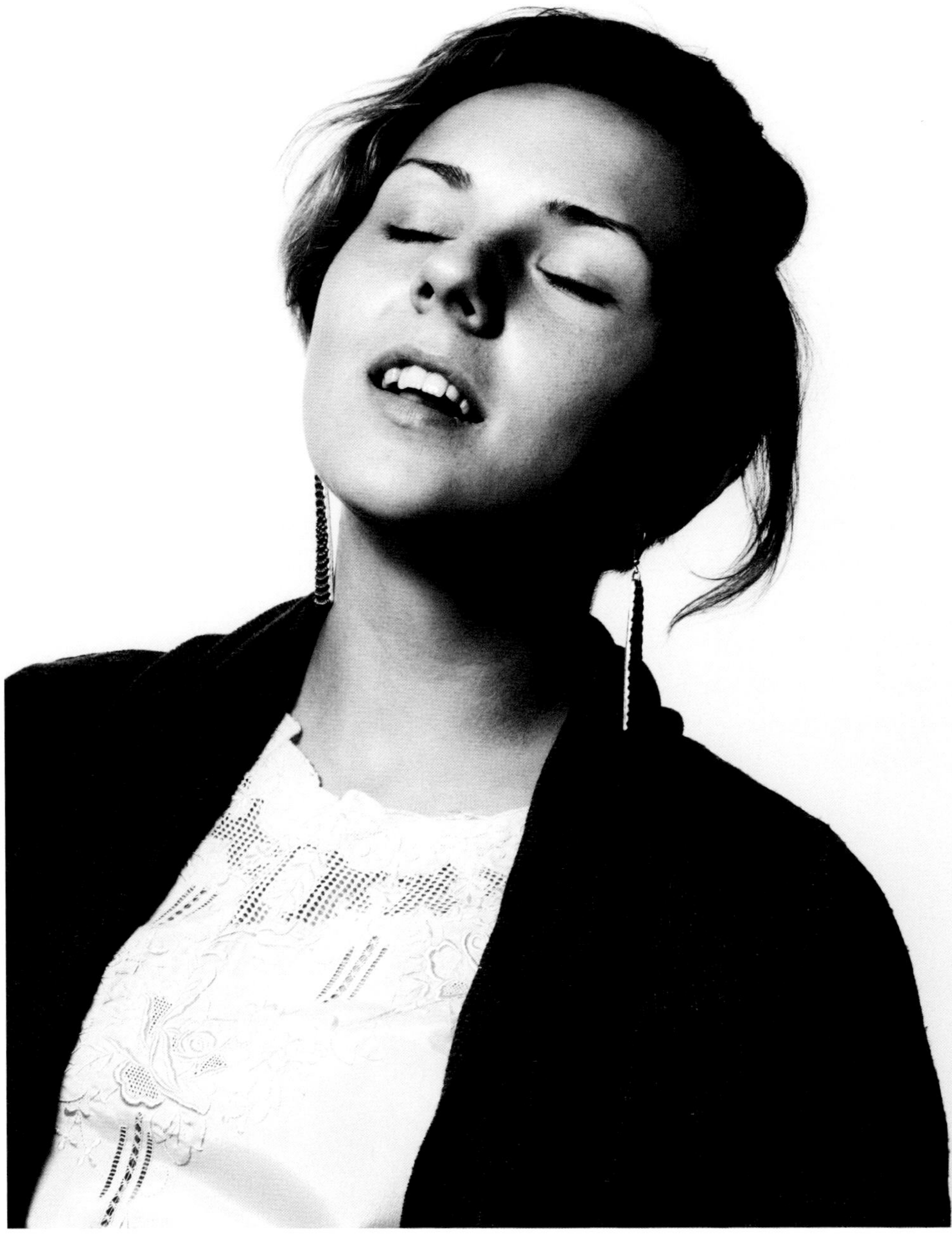

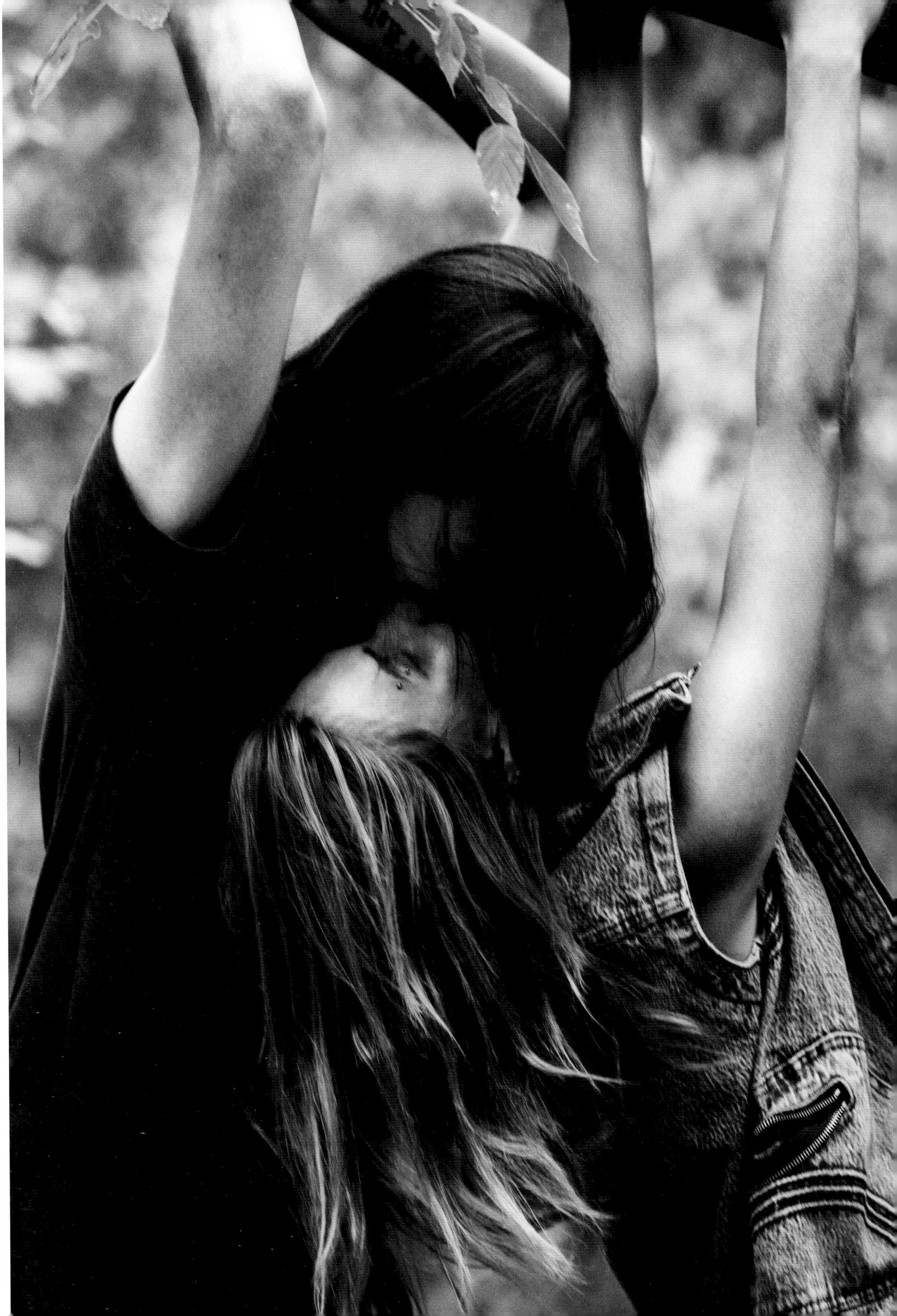

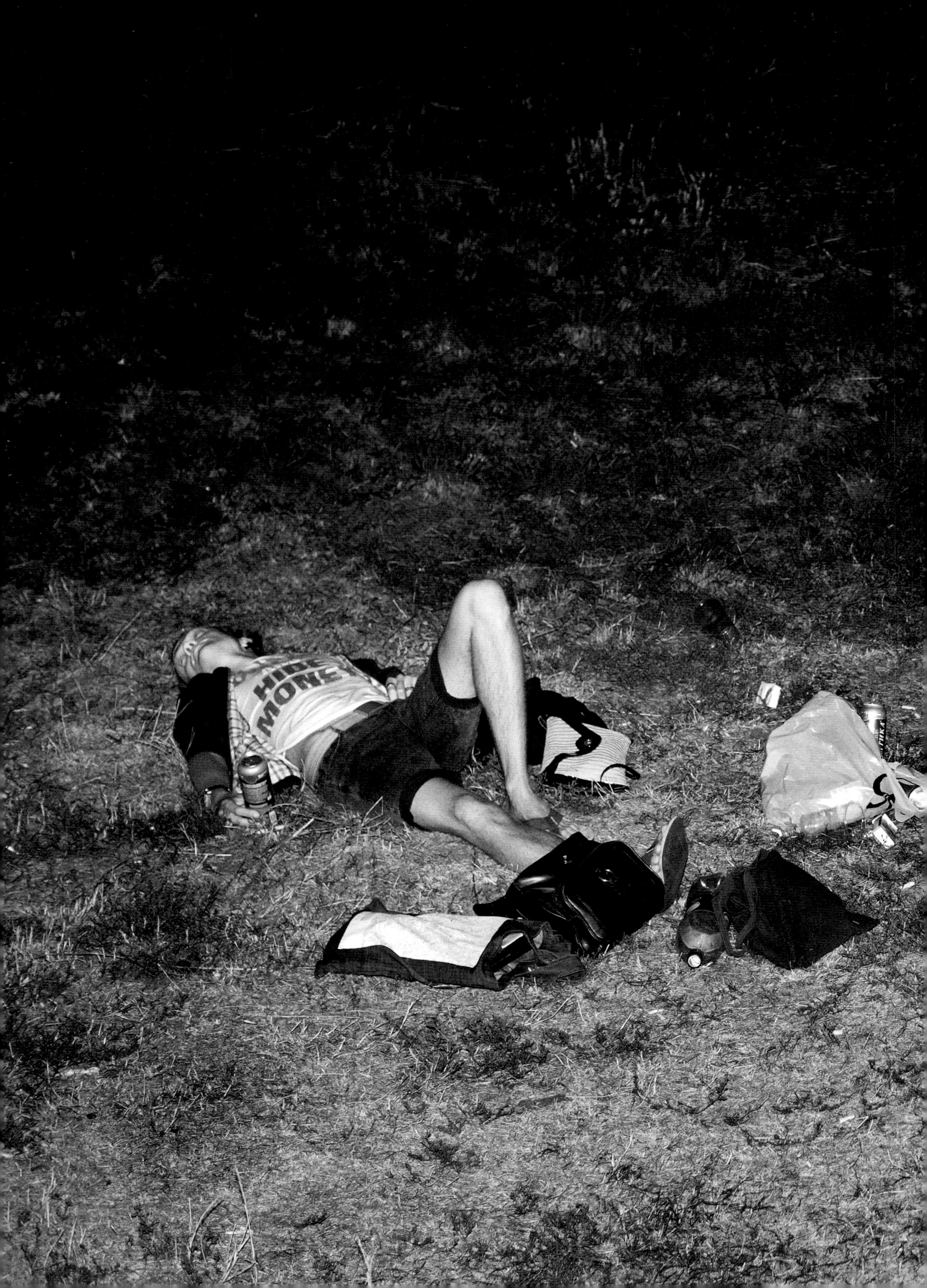

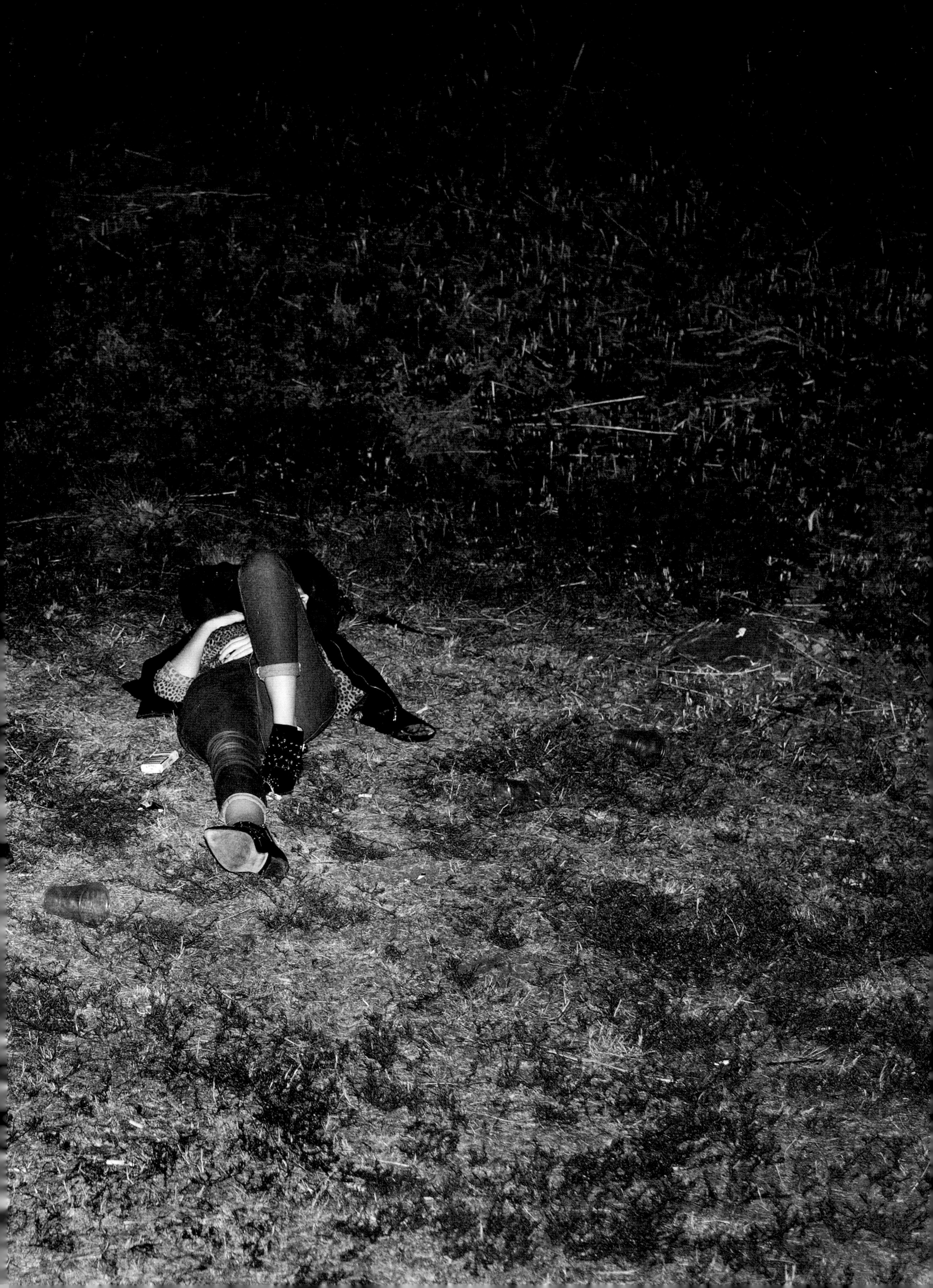

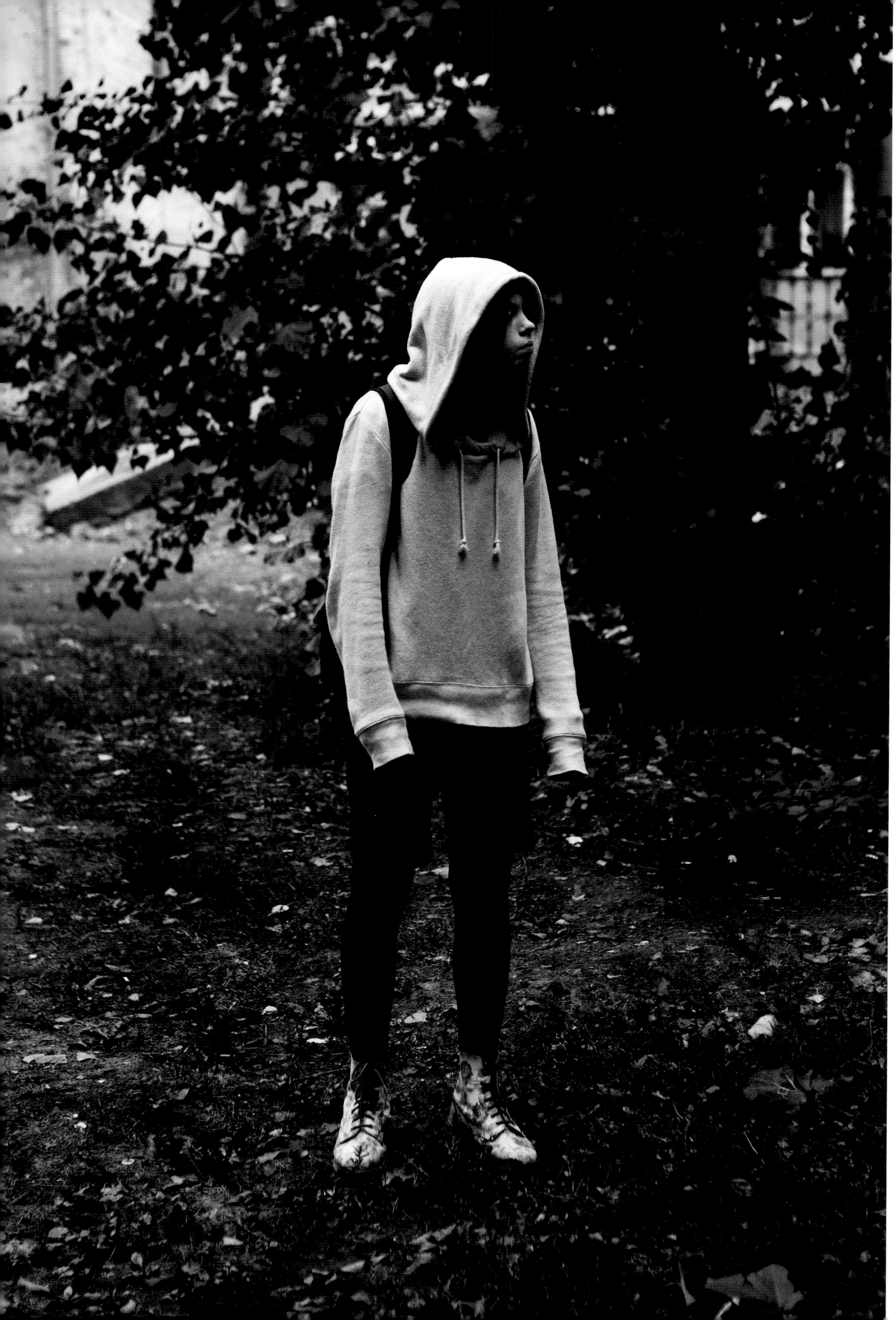

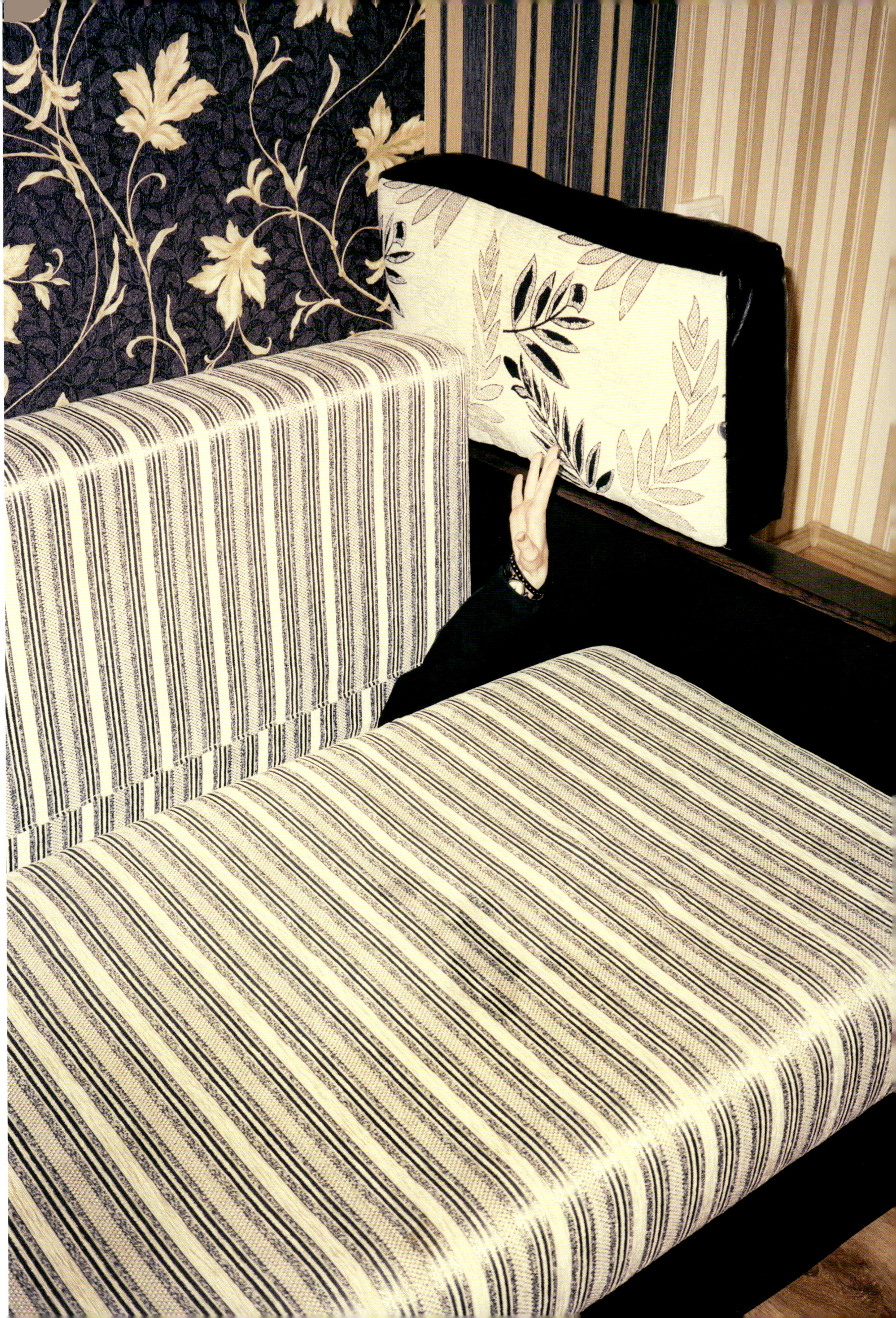

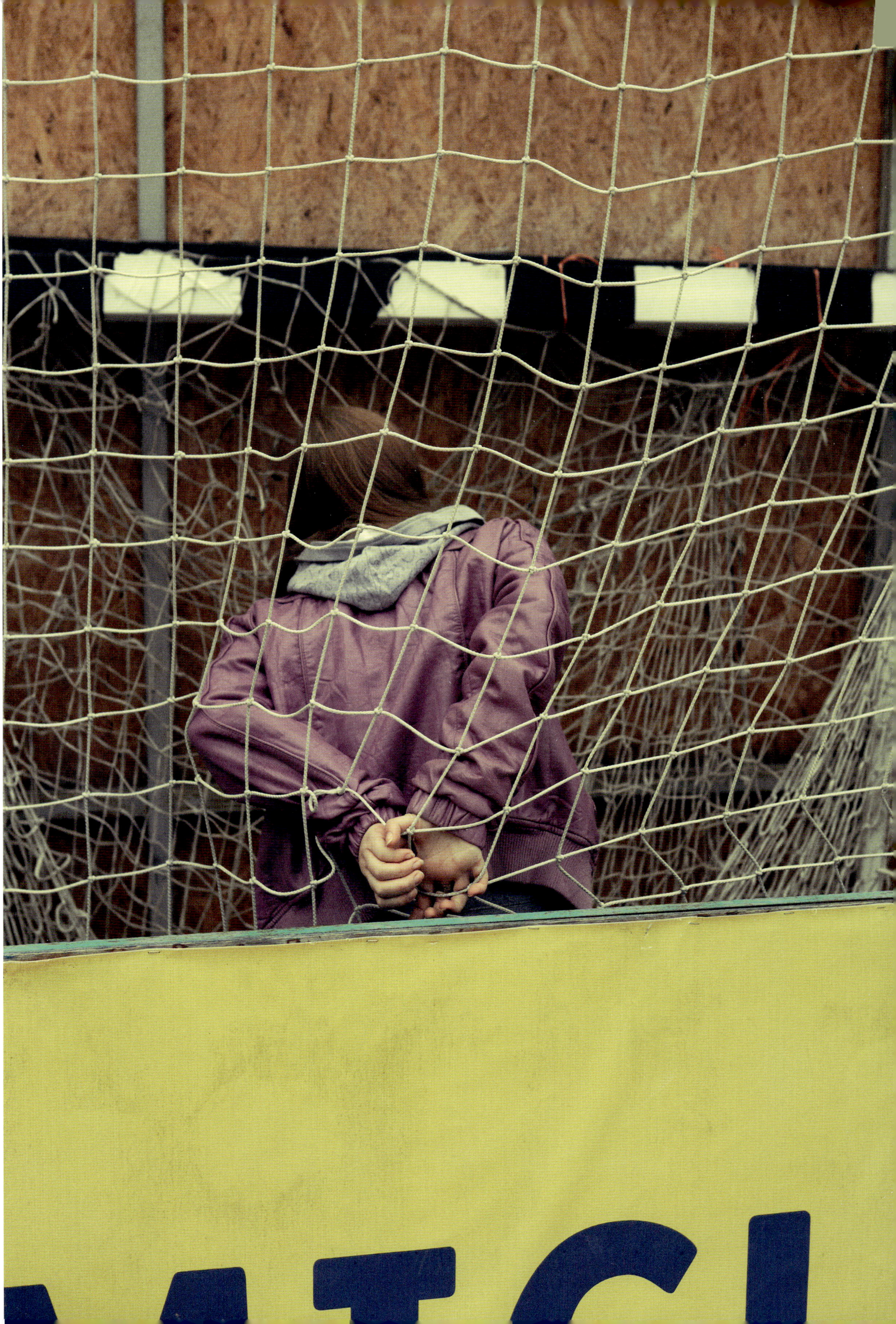

Daniel King
Ukraine Youth Between Days

© Damiani 2015
© Photographs, Daniel King
© Text, Christopher Niquet

Book Design by David Schnapper

DAMIANI

Damiani
Bologna, Italy
info@damianieditore.com
www.damianieditore.com

All rights reserved. No part of this publication may be reproduced or transmitted in any form or by any means, electronic or mechanical – including photocopying, recording or by any information storage or retrieval system – without prior permission in writing from the publisher.

Printed in January 2015 by Grafiche Damiani, Italy.

ISBN 978-88-6208-398-0